Managing
Lease
Portfolios

Managing Lease Portfolios

How to Increase Return and Control Risk

TOWNSEND WALKER

John Wiley & Sons, Inc.

Published by John Wiley & Sons, Inc., Hoboken, New Jersey.
Published simultaneously in Canada.

For general information on our other products and services or for technical support, please contact our Customer Care Department within the United States at (800) 762-2974, outside the United States at (317) 572-3993 or fax (317) 572-4002.

Designations used by companies to distinguish their products are often claimed by trademarks. In all instances where the author or publisher is aware of a claim, the product names appear in Initial Capital letters. Readers, however, should contact the appropriate companies for more complete information regarding trademarks and registration.

Wiley also publishes its books in a variety of electronic formats. Some content that appears in print may not be available in electronic books. For more information about Wiley products, visit our web site at www.wiley.com.

Library of Congress Cataloging-in-Publication Data:
Walker, Townsend, 1942–
 Managing lease portfolios : how to increase income and control risk / Townsend Walker.
  p. cm.—(Wiley finance series)
 Includes bibliographical references.
 ISBN-13: 978-0-471-70630-4 (cloth)
 ISBN-10: 0-471-70630-2 (cloth)
 1. Leases. 2. Office equipment leases. 3. Industrial equipment leases. 4. Lease and rental services—Management. 5. Portfolio management. 6. Risk management. I. Title. I. Series.
 HD39.4.W33 2006
 658.15'242—dc22

                                                              2005012267

Printed in the United States of America.

10 9 8 7 6 5 4 3 2 1

To
Stormy

Contents

Preface

The book has three themes. The first is that you can increase your return and control your risk if the quantifiable elements of a decision are put into a well-conceived model that produces understandable and useable results. The second theme is that an average doesn't tell you a lot. The average of a series of used truck prices or the average default probability is not informative. When thinking about risk you need to know what the range of possibilities is—you need to give the average a context. Context gives you realism. The third theme is that a model does not make the decision; the final decision is a marriage between a disciplined model, measured results, and experience.

Many of the ideas and concepts in this book have existed for a number of years in the fields of foreign exchange, interest rate and credit derivatives, and the bond and stock markets. The book borrows many of these concepts and configures them for leases. Then it shows how to implement the concepts in concrete models you can use. The important concepts are expressed three ways—in words, pictures, and equations.

This book gives leasing people a set of tools that will enable them to manage their businesses more comfortably and confidently. The intention is that the tools be easy and practical, both to implement and to use. All of the tools can be created and tested in MS Excel, with a Monte Carlo simulation add-in, on a laptop. Links to other in-house or external programs would require more extensive programming, as would a fully specified portfolio model.

My suggestion is to go through the book lightly the first time, look for ideas you want to work with, then go back and use it as a reference guide to implement the ideas. Ultimately it is designed as a reference book. The first chapter is an introduction to leases, primarily for those who come to the subject from outside the leasing industry. For those in the leasing business, it offers a look at leases as a bundle of cash flows, with attendant risks and returns.

Chapters 2, 3, and 5 look at the principal risks in leasing—equipment, credit, and tax—with emphasis on thinking about risks as they evolve over the life of a lease. Models are developed to measure the risks over time. Chapter 4 develops a risk pricing tool for leases, which incorporates (1) equipment risk over time and at the end of a lease; (2) probability of default of the lessee and changes in the probability over time; and (3) the variability of recoveries from defaulting lessees. The analysis is extended to estimate the return on risk-adjusted capital over the life of a lease.

Chapter 6 is about the options embedded in a lease, how to calculate their value, and how much you should be charging lessees for the options. Chapter 7 pulls on themes initiated in Chapter 1: How much return are you earning, on an individual risk basis for the risk you are taking in the lease?

Chapter 8 is about diversification—how to identify it, how to measure it, and how diversification can change. Chapter 9 extends the diversification theme and shows how the economic factors underlying lessee credit and equipment can be tracked to prices and become early warning indicators of trouble.

The path of the book starts with a single lease, goes on in Chapter 8 to explain how leases go together, then in Chapter 10 discusses what leases look like in a portfolio setting. A portfolio model gathers the risks and returns that have been measured on individual leases and their individual return and risk components and shows how to put them together into a portfolio that today and in the future will give you the highest income stream for the amount of risk you are willing to take. This chapter also addresses how much risk you may want to take.

Chapter 11 shows what you can do with the risks you have if you wish to eliminate or reduce them. There are a number of possible candidates for risk reduction in the market. The ones included in this chapter are those that are most commonly implemented. The last chapter, on the portfolio management function, puts all the tools into an organizational context.

The Bibliography contains only references that span more than one of the topics in the book. References to specific subjects are contained in the Notes for each chapter.

Many of the ideas and models presented here saw their first light at conferences and workshops sponsored by The Leasing Exchange and the Equipment Leasing Association. My thanks to these organizations for the opportunity, and to the attendees for their comments on the material.

I was introduced to leasing at Bank of America and had the opportunity to learn from a number of people and test out some ideas and models. The environment was encouraging and everyone was most willing to share their knowledge and opinions. While working at Bank of America and APERIMUS I have encountered a number of people at other companies who are singled out here for what they shared about leasing and how to approach problems of uncertainty—Bill Carpenter, Jim Jordan, Bill Kusack, Mark Lundin, Mary Maier, Sue Noack, Lisa Busca Pinheiro, Bob Purcell, and Sam Savage.

Three people stand out for their contributions to my knowledge and how I think about leasing and finance: Beverly Davis, who has a wisdom and vision of how the portfolio management process works and employs these qualities successfully every day; Ron Ginochio, who is one of the best minds in combining finance and leasing in a practical fashion; and Chuck Sellman, my partner at APERIMUS for four years. Together we created a number of tools to make risk and return measurement in leasing an easy, everyday thing. Thank you.

Beverly Mills read the entire manuscript. She tracked the logic of the arguments, saw the hidden assumptions, and brought them to light. The book flows with greater clarity and continuity as a result of her contributions.

Any errors are my responsibility.

TOWNSEND WALKER

Rome
June 2005

Managing
Lease
Portfolios

CHAPTER 1

What a Lease Looks Like

This chapter is an introduction to leases. One aim is to provide sufficient information about leases for those unfamiliar with them, but more importantly, the purpose is to orient you to a particular way of looking at a lease—as a bundle of cash flows that provides a return to the leasing company, with each cash flow changing in importance over time, and each cash flow being subject to certain risks.

REASONS TO LEASE RATHER THAN BUY

According to a recent survey[1] three of the main reasons a company leases equipment rather than buying it are:

1. Leasing equipment protects companies against owning equipment that may become technologically obsolete—that risk is shifted to the lessor.
2. Often the company does not have to show the equipment and the debt financing it on its balance sheet. On their face, the financials of the company leasing the equipment look better than they otherwise would.
3. The company leasing the equipment cannot make use of the depreciation benefits.

CHARACTERISTICS OF A LEASE

A lease is a contract that lets a company (lessee) rent equipment for a specified period of time. The rent is paid periodically throughout the term of the lease—every month, or every 3, 6, or 12 months. The leasing company (lessor) owns the equipment.

Lessors deduct the depreciation charges for the equipment from their income before calculating their taxes. Lessees receive part of the tax benefit of depreciation in the form of lower rent.

How a Lease Works

The way a lease works can be described in five steps:

1. A company needs new equipment. It specifies the make, model, and features, and negotiates the price with the manufacturer.
2. The company then negotiates an agreement with a lessor—how much rent, for how long, and what the equipment will be worth at the end of the lease.
3. The equipment is delivered. The company and the lessor make sure it is what was ordered. The lessor pays for it.
4. Rent payments are made by the company, now a lessee, to the lessor.
5. At the end of the lease the lessee may have an option to renew the lease or to buy the equipment.

WHY LEASING IS DIFFERENT

Leasing is unique in three fundamental ways:

1. The lessor owns the equipment and is not simply financing it. In most cases, a lessor buys a piece of equipment only when it has a customer who wants to use it. In the case of airplanes and rail cars, however, there are leasing companies that order planes and rail cars without specific customer orders in the hope they will be able to lease the equipment when it is delivered.
2. Leases are long. Though a computer lease probably lasts no more than three years, the lease on a rail car may last up to 25 years, and the lease on a power plant for 30 years. This means that at the start of the lease it is not easy to take into account everything that can happen to the equipment or to the lessee for the next 3 to 30 years.
3. There is no organized market for buying and selling leases. Leases are not traded like bonds or stocks because there are not

enough common characteristics among them. Lease prices do not show up on Bloomberg or Reuters. There is a reasonably active private market for syndicating leases when they are originated. Sales of seasoned leases (2 to 10 years old), however, are not common, so if a lessor is unhappy with the risk or return on a lease it has in portfolio, it may take a while to fix the problem. This lack of a ready market means that the lessor must be careful when deciding what leases it wants in portfolio and have the tools for tracking what is happening with the lessee, the equipment, and tax rates and regulations.

ATTRACTIONS OF A LEASE TO A LESSOR

Four distinct advantages make a lease attractive to a lessor:

1. Regular cash flow from the rent payments.
2. The prospect of making a profit on selling the equipment when the lease is over.
3. Tax benefits of depreciation on the equipment.
4. Ability to further enhance the value of a lease with a creative financial structuring.

However, that which is valued is always at risk against a change in the value. The sources of value to the lessor are sources of risk—the lessee can stop paying rent, the equipment may not be worth very much at the end of the lease, the depreciation may not be as valuable as was calculated at the start of the lease, or the structure turns out to be overly aggressive when viewed later by tax and accounting auditors.

SETTING THE RENT ON A LEASE

Five things are taken into consideration when determining the amount of rent:

1. The value of the equipment today and what it will be worth at the end of the lease.
2. The likelihood the lessee may stop paying the rent.

3. The value of being able to take depreciation on the equipment.
4. The cost to the lessor of borrowing the money to buy the equipment.
5. The amount the lessor needs to charge, and keep in reserve, to cover the risk of getting the preceding four estimates wrong.

DIFFERENT KINDS OF LEASES

There are four basic kinds of leases:

1. *Single investor leases.* This is the most common type of lease. The lessor supplies all of the money to buy the equipment. The length of the lease cannot be more than 80 percent of the useful life of the equipment to be eligible for tax treatment. The rent paid by the lessee is set by taking into account rental payments, depreciation, and the value of the equipment at the end of the original lease term. Because of the value of the depreciation tax benefits and the lease end value of the equipment, the rental payments are generally lower than interest and principal payments on a similar loan. The lessor monitors the ability of the lessee to pay rent and is concerned about the value of the equipment at lease end, as well as the value of the tax benefits.
2. *Leveraged leases.* The principal difference from a single investor lease is that the lessor supplies less than the entire cost of the equipment, an equity portion of somewhere between 20 percent and 40 percent. Lenders (commercial banks and insurance companies) provide the rest as debt. The lessor receives the tax benefits and resale rights from owning the equipment, but is not responsible to the lenders for paying off the debt in the event the lessee stops paying rent. On the other hand, the lessor is second in the pecking order in the event the lessee goes bankrupt. The lenders have first rights to the proceeds from selling the equipment plus additional proceeds from the lessee's estate. Leveraged leases are generally used for longer-lived and larger types of equipment. The benefits of this structure are greater and they cost more to put together.

3. *Operating leases.* The principal difference between an operating lease and the others is that its length is substantially shorter than the useful life of the equipment. Equipment like airplanes and rail cars can have 25- to 30-year lives. A lessor buys them and rents them out five to seven years at a time. The lessor usually supplies all the money to buy the equipment. Though the lessor monitors the ability of the lessee to make rent payments, the lessor is less concerned, relative to other leases, because it owns equipment that is a commodity and it can easily be leased to someone else. The principal problems operating lessors face are industry downturns, not individual lessee difficulties.

4. *TRAC leases.* TRAC stands for "terminal rental adjustment clause." These leases are limited by law to over-the-road vehicles—tractors, trucks, buses, and auto fleets. The principal difference with this type of lease is that the lessor bears no risk on the equipment at the end of the lease. A terminal value is agreed to at the beginning of the lease. If the vehicle sells for more than that value, the lessee gets a rebate on its rent; if it sells for less, the lessee pays the lessor the difference.

Table 1.1, on page 6, summarizes the principal distinctions among leases. The last column in the chart is about risk. In this book, risk means uncertainty. When looking at the future we generally have some idea about the way things (prices, values) will end up—on average. Measures of risk tell us about the range and clustering of future prices around the average. Is there a small chance of a large positive result, or a large chance of a large negative outcome? Chapter 2 defines risk in more specific statistical terms.

LEASES AS A SET OF CASH FLOWS

The last column of Table 1.1 is the focus of this book—how to get a better handle on measuring the risks of a lease and the return you are getting for taking those risks. One of the first steps in that process is to break a lease into cash flow streams that are

TABLE 1.1 Differences among Types of Leases

Type of Lease	How Long Do They Last?	Who Supplies the Money to Buy the Equipment?	Who Gets the Tax Benefits of Owning the Equipment?	Who Owns the Equipment at the End of the Lease?	What Is at Risk for the Lessor?
Single Investor	80 percent of the useful life of equipment	Lessor	Lessor	Lessor	Rent Equipment value Tax benefits
Leveraged	80 percent of the useful life of equipment	Lessor and lenders	Lessor	Lessor	Rent after debt service Position in bankruptcy Equipment value Tax benefits
Operating	Shorter than the useful life of equipment	Lessor	Lessor	Lessor	Equipment value Tax benefits
TRAC	80 percent of the useful life of equipment	Lessor	Lessor	Lessee	Rent Tax benefits

generated by the different elements in a lease. Understanding them and their interaction will enable you to manage them better.

Table 1.2 shows the principal cash flows of a single investor lease from the point of view of the lessor.[2] The equipment cost $1,000,000 and is bought on January 1, 2005. It is depreciated over five years. Only federal taxes of 35 percent are calculated. You do not need to look at the details of the calculations, only notice certain characteristics of the cash flows.

- In the "Taxable Income" column, the lessor's taxable income is negative in the first three years of the lease because depreciation is greater than rent in these years. The lessor or its parent company is able to deduct this amount from other income before calculating income taxes.
- In the "Taxes" column the effect of the depreciation is evident—the lessor saves $75,000 in taxes in the first three years, and it's not until year six of the lease that it pays any taxes on a net basis.
- If you look at the total of "Pre-Tax Cash Flow" (unaffected by depreciation) and the total of "Taxes," you'll see that the lessor pays a 35 percent tax rate. Depreciation doesn't eliminate the tax bill, it pushes it off into the future. And that is valuable.
- Note the difference between the "After-Tax Cash Flow" series and the "Accounting Income" series. They total to the same number but are very different in timing. This is due to the accounting conventions governing leases. Income for accounting purposes is computed by calculating the amount the lessor has invested in the lease in any year, and multiplying that amount by the rate on the transaction. This is, as is evident, very different than the pattern of the way cash is received by the lessor. In this book we'll focus primarily on the economic risks of the transactions.
- The "Termination Value" column shows what the lessor has at risk any year during the lease. It includes the rents to be paid, equipment value, and the value of taxes that have been deferred. In a single investor lease the termination value decreases as time goes on.

TABLE 1.2 Cash Flows of a 10-Year Single Investor Lease

Year Ending Dec. 31	Purchase and Residual	Rent	Pre-Tax Cash Flow	Depreciation	Taxable Income	Taxes	After-Tax Cash Flow	Accounting Income	Termination Value
1/1/2005	(1,000,000)		(1,000,000)				(1,000,000)		1,000,000
2005	0	166,010	166,010	(200,000)	(33,990)	(11,896)	177,906	75,484	1,000,000
2006	0	166,010	166,010	(320,000)	(153,990)	(53,896)	219,906	74,134	961,028
2007	0	166,010	166,010	(192,000)	(25,990)	(9,096)	175,106	63,328	907,575
2008	0	166,010	166,010	(115,200)	50,810	17,784	148,226	54,826	837,846
2009	0	166,010	166,010	(115,200)	50,810	17,784	148,226	47,073	755,225
2010	0	135,827	135,827	(57,600)	78,227	27,379	108,448	38,954	660,597
2011	0	135,827	135,827		135,827	47,539	88,288	33,552	583,679
2012	0	135,827	135,827		135,827	47,539	88,288	29,010	498,909
2013	0	135,827	135,827		135,827	47,539	88,288	24,089	407,103
2014	0	135,827	135,827		135,827	47,539	88,288	18,760	307,678
12/31/14	200,000		200,000		200,000	70,000	130,000	1,760	200,000
Totals	(800,000)	1,709,183	709,185	(1,000,000)	709,185	248,214	460,970	460,970	

Legend: Rent—payments made by the lessee. Pre-tax cash flow—purchase of the equipment plus rent plus the residual.
Depreciation—schedule specific to the equipment type. Taxable income—rent minus depreciation. Taxes—35% of taxable income.
After-tax cash flow—pre-tax cash flow minus taxes. Accounting income—defined by accounting regulations.
Termination value—amount in any year needed to make the lessor whole in the event the lessee defaults.

CONTRIBUTIONS OF RENT, EQUIPMENT, AND TAXES

One way of looking at the changing contributions over time is to calculate the present value of the remaining cash flows each year. This number will give you a picture of what is important today and the change in importance over time. It's as if you were walking along in time and were able to take a look at what you cared about most each year. Figure 1.1 shows the changes in rent, equipment, and tax contributions.

- As time goes on, the contribution of equipment increases because the day the equipment is coming back to the lessor becomes closer.
- The cash received by the lessor (rent) is the most important consideration in the lease up until the last couple of years, though it declines as the rent payments are made.
- Taxes that had been deferred are paid toward the end of the lease.

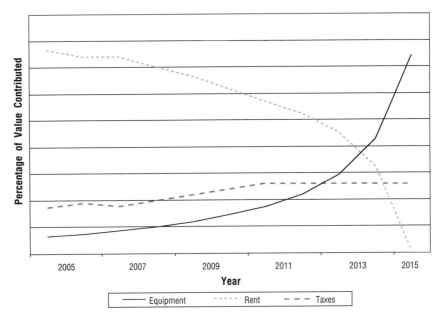

FIGURE 1.1 Importance of Cash Flows over Time for a Single Investor Lease

TABLE 1.3 Cash Flows of a 20-Year Leveraged Lease

Year Ending Dec. 31	Purchase, Loan, and Residual	Rent	Principal	Interest	Pre-Tax Cash Flow	Depreciation	Taxable Income	Taxes	After-Tax Cash Flow	Accounting Income	Termination Value
1/1/2005	(1,000,000) 774,686				(225,314)				(225,314)		
2005		79,036	(17,061)	(61,975)		(142,857)	(125,796)	(44,029)	44,029	15,815	225,314
2006		79,036	(18,426)	(60,610)		(244,898)	(226,472)	(79,265)	79,265	14,072	251,666
2007		79,036	(19,900)	(59,136)		(174,927)	(155,027)	(54,259)	54,259	9,383	272,647
2008		79,036	(21,492)	(57,544)		(124,948)	(103,456)	(36,210)	36,209	6,179	286,622
2009		79,036	(23,212)	(55,825)		(89,249)	(66,037)	(23,113)	23,113	4,064	295,820
2010		79,036	(25,069)	(53,968)		(89,249)	(64,180)	(22,463)	22,463	2,502	301,877
2011		79,036	(27,074)	(51,962)		(89,249)	(62,174)	(21,761)	21,761	865	305,521
2012		79,036	(29,240)	(49,796)		(44,624)	(15,384)	(5,385)	5,385	0	306,668
2013		79,036	(28,798)	(47,457)	2,782	0	31,579	11,053	(8,271)	0	306,668
2014		79,036	(21,601)	(45,153)	12,283	0	33,883	11,859	423	361	303,915
2015		96,600	(33,899)	(43,425)	19,276	0	53,175	18,611	665	618	292,284
2016		96,600	(35,628)	(40,713)	20,259	0	55,887	19,560	698	692	274,031
2017		96,600	(37,445)	(37,863)	21,292	0	58,737	20,558	734	727	254,846
2018		96,600	(41,768)	(34,867)	19,965	0	61,733	21,606	(1,642)	764	234,684
2019		96,600	(65,074)	(31,526)		0	65,074	22,776	(22,776)	988	215,906
2020		96,600	(70,280)	(26,320)		0	70,280	24,598	(24,598)	2,870	217,465
2021		96,600	(75,902)	(20,698)		0	75,902	26,566	(26,566)	5,207	222,162
2022		96,600	(81,974)	(14,625)		0	81,974	28,691	(28,691)	7,905	230,499
2023		96,600	(88,532)	(8,067)		0	88,532	30,986	(30,986)	11,009	243,036
2024		96,600	(12,311)	(985)	83,305	0	95,615	33,465	49,839	14,566	260,403
12/31/2024	200,000				200,000		200,000	70,000	130,000	1,413	200,000
Totals	(800,000)	1,756,360	(774,686)	(802,514)	153,846	(1,000,000)	153,846	53,846	100,000	100,000	

Legend: Rent—payments made by the lessee. Principal—payments made from rent to the lender to pay down the principal of the loan. Interest—paid to the lender on the loan. Pre-tax cash flow—purchase of the equipment plus rent minus principle minus interest plus the residual. Depreciation—schedule specific to the equipment type. Taxable income—rent plus residual minus depreciation and minus interest. Taxes—35% of taxable income. After-tax cash flow—pre-tax cash flow minus taxes. Accounting income—defined by accounting regulations. Termination value—amount in any year needed to make the lessor whole in the event the lessee defaults.

The composition of risks that affect the lessor's return is shifting as the importance of the value streams shifts. This is one of the dynamics of the lease. The other dynamic is that the nature of the risks themselves shifts as time goes on.

DIFFERENCES BETWEEN A LEVERAGED LEASE AND A SINGLE INVESTOR LEASE

The introduction of a lender into the lease structure changes the dynamics and interactions of the cash flows from the perspective of the lessor. The changes are most easily tracked by looking at the cash flows of a leveraged lease. Table 1.3 illustrates a 20-year leveraged lease. The assumptions are that the equipment costs $1 million today and it will be worth $200,000 at the end of 20 years. The lease starts on January 1, 2005. The equipment is depreciated over seven years. The lessor puts in $225,314 in equity; the remainder is borrowed from a bank. As in the previous example, you do not need to look at the details of the calculations, only notice certain characteristics of the cash flows.

- In the "Taxable Income" column, the lessor's taxable income is negative in the first eight years of the lease. (It was three years for the single investor lease.) This is because depreciation and interest are greater than rent in these years. The lessor or its parent can deduct this amount from other income before calculating income taxes.
- In the "Taxes" column the effect of the depreciation is evident— the lessor saves $286,000 in taxes in the first eight years, and it's not until the last year of the lease that it pays any taxes on a net basis.
- If you look at the total of "Pre-Tax Cash Flow" (unaffected by depreciation) and the total of "Taxes," you'll see that the lessor pays a 35 percent tax rate. Again, depreciation doesn't eliminate the tax bill, it pushes it off into the future. With a leveraged lease the delay is even more dramatic than with a single investor lease, even adjusting for the difference in tenors of the examples.

- Looking at "After-Tax Cash Flow" and "Accounting Income" you can see, as with the single investor lease, a significant difference between economics and accounting due to the accounting convention for leases, though the difference is not as great as with the single investor lease. Focusing on the accounting results often distorts the view of what the underlying economics are, sometimes hiding the economics from view, which in turn prompts people to take actions to improve accounting results, but not for risk or economics. Figure 1.2 compares the cash flow and accounting results.
- The significant difference between leveraged leases and single investor leases is in the lessor's exposure to risk, and its ability to do something about it. Note in the "Termination Value" column that the amount at risk increases for eight years before starting to decline. And because of the contractual arrangements with the lessee and lender, the lessor is last in line in the event the lessee cannot pay.

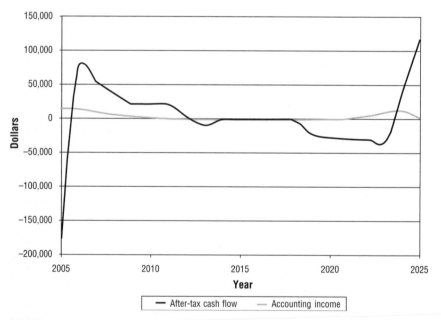

FIGURE 1.2   After-Tax Cash Flow and Accounting Income

FACTORS THAT CONTRIBUTE TO LEASE VALUE

A couple of calculations will make it easier to see what is happening to the values of rent, equipment, and taxes from the start throughout the lease. Figure 1.3 shows the present value of the cash flow streams as a percent of total cash flows over time for each year of the lease. As in the single investor example, you are walking through time to see what the values look like every year.

- As time goes on the contribution of Equipment increases, as the day the equipment comes back to the leasing company draws nearer.
- The lessor does not receive any cash until the eighth year of the lease and then some at the end. This is reflected in the chart. The importance of the cash (rent less debt service) increases up to the time it comes in, falls off, and then increases slightly. Compared to Figure 1.1, the single investor lease, cash is much less important.

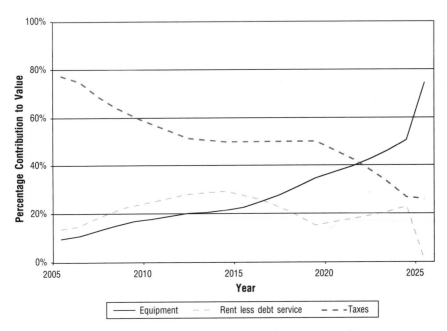

FIGURE 1.3   Importance of Cash Flows over Time for a Leveraged Lease

- Tax benefits are the driver for a leveraged lease. Compare Figure 1.3 to Figure 1.1. The reason for the dominance of the tax flow is that even though the lessor puts up only 25 percent of the money to buy the equipment, it takes 100 percent of the equipment depreciation and deducts the interest on the debt. As with the single investor lease, the composition of risks that affect the lessor's return is shifting as the importance of the value streams is shifting.

The position of the lessor relative to the lender affects both the amount of rent the lessor receives and the ability of the lessor to recover the equipment in the event of lessee default. In Figure 1.4, look at the relative positions of the lessor and lender during most of the lease. The lender has a larger and superior position. It has first claim on proceeds if the deal unwinds. Only as the loan is repaid toward the end of the lease does the lessor's share begin to exceed 40 percent.

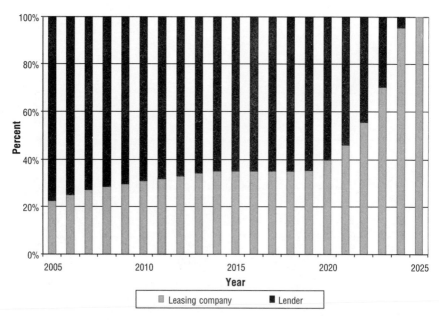

FIGURE 1.4   Positions of Lessor and Lender in a Leveraged Lease

TABLE 1.4 Your Lease Portfolio

Equipment	Lessee	Credit Rating	Type of Lease	Start Date	End Date	After-Tax Yield	Residual	Leverage
Boeing 737-800 aircraft	Ryanair	Not rated	Operating	2006	2011	6.00%	50%	NA
Case G series forklifts	Shamrock Foods	Not rated	Single investor	2007	2011	5.50%	15%	NA
Trinity Industries gondola rail cars	CSX	BBB	Leveraged	2001	2020	5.70%	25%	75%
GE DASH9 locomotives	SNCF	AAA	Leveraged	1989	2014	7.50%	25%	75%
Van Dorn Demag Multi molding machines	Ningbo Fortune Plastic	Not rated	Single investor	2001	2008	5.75%	15%	NA
Lufkin high cube van trailers	JB Hunt	BBB+	Single investor	2003	2010	4.00%	20%	NA
Mack Granite series trucks	R & J Contractors	Not rated	Single investor	2003	2010	6.00%	15%	NA
Timsons T48 book presses	RR Donnelley	A-	Single investor	2005	2015	5.00%	15%	NA
Coal-fired electricity plant, 994 MW	Calpine	B	Leveraged	1995	2025	8.00%	25%	80%
Sun Fire E12K and E25K servers	Amazon	B+	Single investor	2006	2010	8.00%	5%	NA
Oracle application servers	Fifth Third Bancorp	AA	Single investor	2005	2009	7.50%	5%	NA

YOUR LEASE PORTFOLIO

The purpose of this book is to help you learn how to apply various financial tools toward managing leases; therefore, you will need something at hand to apply the tools to. Table 1.4, on page 15, shows the details of your sample portfolio. As we look at ways to measure the risks of a lease, calculate their returns, estimate the effects of diversification, and think about managing a portfolio, we will apply them to this portfolio.[3]

CHAPTER 2

Equipment Risk

In Chapter 1, Figures 1.1 and 1.3 show the importance of equipment value to the value of the lease. It follows that when calculating the return on a lease, the estimate of future equipment value is critical. In most cases the value of the equipment will decline, but you need to know by how much and how fast. Being wrong about the estimate significantly impacts the return on the lease. Figure 2.1 is an illustration of three leases of different maturities (3, 5, and 10 years); the same amount ($1,000,000); and the same initial estimate of equipment value at lease end ($200,000). The individual rent schedules plus the lease end equipment estimate result in the same scheduled return on capital (15 percent) for each of the leases. Additional assumptions are a tax rate of 35 percent and loss reserves of 2.5 percent; $900,000 of debt and $100,000 of capital are used to buy the equipment initially; the cost of debt for all maturities is 7 percent.

However, if the equipment is sold at lease end for only $150,000, on a 3-year lease the return falls to nearly zero; on a 5-year lease the return on capital is reduced to 7 percent; and on a 10-year lease the return on capital is reduced to 10 percent. Clearly, the effect of overestimating the equipment value at lease end has a major impact on profitability.

Equipment risk also exists during the lease. Every lessor expects some percentage of its lessees will default on their lease payments. These expectations are built into the rents charged in the lease, and a portion of the rents is reserved for this default contingency. Proceeds from the sale of leased equipment are the primary source of recoveries when a lessee defaults on its rent payments. If the value of the

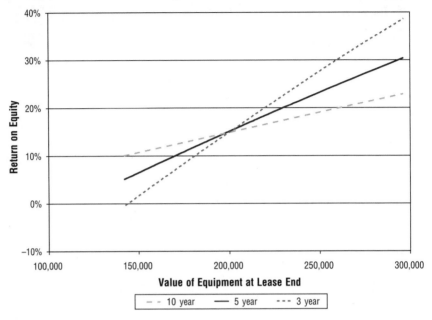

FIGURE 2.1   Comparison of Return on Capital and Value of Equipment

equipment is lower than anticipated, reserves will be insufficient and the lessor will lose money.

The amount of money the lessor has at risk changes over time. The change depends on two things:

1. The number of rent payments that have been made. In general, the more rent payments made, the less money at risk.
2. The type of lease—single investor or leveraged. The single investor lease follows the first principle, but the leveraged lease does not. The amount the lessor has at risk, the termination value, grows before declining.

The next two figures illustrate these points using two leases in your portfolio: the Mack truck lease to R & J Contractors (Figure 2.2) and the locomotive lease to SNCF (Figure 2.3). The estimate of the gradual depreciation of the trucks is shown by the black line in Figure 2.2, while the gray line represents the amount you have at risk. The difference between the black line and the gray line represents what you could lose if R & J Contractors defaults. And this assumes you have estimated the value of the trucks well.

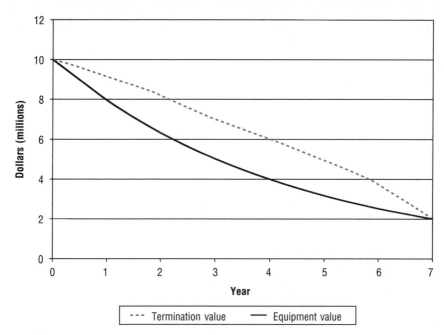

FIGURE 2.2 Equipment Value Compared to Termination Value for a Single Investor Lease

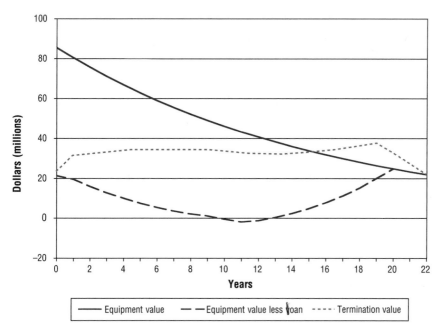

FIGURE 2.3 Equipment Value Compared to Termination Value for a Leveraged Lease

The picture for your lease to SNCF is very different. The estimate of the gradual depreciation of the locomotives is again shown by the solid black line. But more importantly, the dashed black line shows the amount left for you, the lessor—the value of the rail cars less the claim of the lender in the leveraged lease. The gray line represents the amount you have at risk. The difference between the dashed line and the gray line is a representation of what you could lose if SNCF defaults. The amount increases for the first dozen years of the lease before becoming smaller. Again, this assumes you have estimated the value of the locomotives well.

You can be more confident in making estimates of the future value of equipment by combining expert equipment knowledge with statistical techniques.

FACTORS AFFECTING FUTURE EQUIPMENT VALUES

Many things can happen to equipment; most of them are not very predictable. *Physical* factors that affect future equipment values include wear and tear. Equipment wears out as it is used. A five-year-old truck cannot run as long without a visit to the repair shop as a new truck can. The new truck also gets better gas mileage, so the five-year-old truck costs more to operate. *Technical* factors can come into play when an improved piece of equipment is manufactured. A new molding machine produces plastic bottles at twice the speed of the old one; the new 7700 server is four times as fast as model 5800. *Regulatory* factors occur from time to time when the government imposes new standards on equipment, such as reducing the allowable noise from an aircraft engine. At other times government changes the rules of the game—for example, electric utilities are deregulated.

At the *macroeconomic* level, the stage of the business cycle affects the value of everything, including equipment. When the economy is in a recession, fewer people are flying and the values of aircraft are lower. When the economy is expanding, more electricity is being used so power plants are more valuable; more goods are being produced and trucked to the stores, so over-the-road trailers are more valuable.

Demand factors influence future equipment values as people use different equipment to meet traditional needs, like news and communications. Computer screens begin to replace books and newspapers and the demand for printing presses falls.

Price movements are also important influences on value. The prices of inputs and outputs change. When cheese prices are high and milk prices are low, the value of cheese and whey processing equipment goes up. Another example is a manufacturer deciding to increase market share by reducing the price of its new rail cars to just above cost.

Inflation increases the price you can sell equipment for in the future. The effects are fairly powerful. A modest 2.5 percent inflation over 20 years increases prices 64 percent; a 3 percent rate over the same period increases prices 81 percent. When using historical price series to estimate the future, unless you adjust them for inflation, you are projecting the inflation rates of the past into the future.

Political factors would include such things as people not liking the equipment. For example, nuclear power plants fell out of favor after the Chernobyl and Three Mile Island incidents, but these plants begin to look better when the price of oil is high.

Future equipment values can also be affected by *secondary markets*. The number of people that care about a given type of equipment and the amount of that equipment in use influences its value. If there are 100 BAe-146 aircraft remaining in use and only six airlines use them, their value will suffer relative to the 1,100 Boeing 737-300s used by 40 airlines. Another aspect of the secondary market is the ease of moving equipment from its current location to another place. Trucks, airplanes, and forklifts move easily; power plants and plastic molding machinery do not. When it is easy to move equipment, there will be more people interested in buying.

The *lessee*, too, has an effect on the future value of the equipment leased. If the equipment is essential to the operation of the lessee, the lessee will place a high value on it, both during the lease and at lease end. A leased phone system is valued until the lessee finally closes the door on the business. Lessees pay rent on the telephone systems even after declaring bankruptcy. Sometimes the equipment is not essential to the operation of the lessee. This is generally true of a leased corporate jet.

One of the challenges facing lessors is deciding what equipment is essential to the lessee and what is not. There are a few ways of looking at the issue. A lessor's historical records will document the types of equipment purchased by lessees in specific industries at lease end. This "stick rate" is a strong indication of the types of equipment that are essential to lessees' businesses.

You can also look at the income mix of the lessee's business. If a lessee makes 50 percent of its income from supplying transmissions for cars and trucks, 40 percent from building switches and circuit breakers, and 10 percent from producing hydraulic systems, it is reasonable to conclude that the equipment used to manufacture hydraulic systems may not be as essential to the company as the equipment used to make transmissions and switches.

A third approach to the determination of essential equipment is to look at how common a specific type of the equipment is in the business. If the lessee uses the same kind of equipment throughout its business, in a downturn the lessee will place a low value on it. A railroad will not place a high value on the 25 60-foot box cars you have leased to it, if the railroad has 500 of them.

A final factor that affects future equipment values is the *lease contract* itself. The maintenance, use, and return conditions that the lessor and lessee agree to in the lease influence the value of the equipment. A forklift that is used in a covered warehouse moving furniture will be more valuable at the end of the lease than one used on construction sites in Kansas. An airplane returned to the Ezeiza airport in Buenos Aires will be less valuable than one returned to Dallas–Fort Worth.

PRINCIPLES FOR ESTIMATING EQUIPMENT VALUES

There are four principles that should be followed in estimating future equipment values.

Distribution

Estimates of future values should be described in terms of a distribution rather than a point estimate. A distribution is simply an arrangement of values of an estimate showing how often they occur. Figure 2.4 is an example of a distribution of estimated values at lease end of one of the locomotives on lease to SNCF. The different

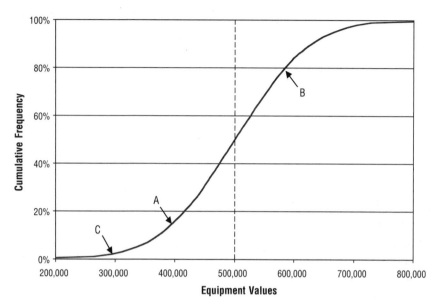

FIGURE 2.4   Distribution of Equipment Values

ways of representing distributions are in the Appendix for this chapter. The estimate can be done for any year during the lease. The average of $500,000 is denoted by the dashed line; but the range of possibilities is from $200,000 to $800,000. This is the risk, the uncertainty; it represents a hazard if it is at the low end of the range, and the gods are smiling if it is at the high end.

The numbers on the vertical axis indicate the probability of each of the values. For example, at point A, 15 percent of the estimated values are below $395,000; 85 percent are greater. If the lease end value is booked at $395,000 there is a 15 percent chance of not being right, and an 85 percent chance of selling the locomotives for at least this amount, or more. If the lease end value is booked at $580,000 (point B), there is an 80 percent chance of not being right, and only a 20 percent chance of selling the locomotives for this amount or more.

The distribution allows you to choose a value that you are comfortable with. Are you willing to be wrong 15 percent of the time at point A, or only 2 percent of the time at point C? Your willingness to take risk affects the future value you incorporate in your lease return calculations.

Sources of Information

Distributions should be generated from more than one source, then compared, and combined where possible. The four possible sources of information are:

1. Historical data from lessors' records.
2. Public source data—for example, Dove Bid, Iron Solutions, Rail Solutions, and Avitas.
3. Producer price indices.
4. Input and output factors that affect the value of the equipment. For example, the volatility of the value of a refinery might be estimated with a crack spread series—the price of gasoline less the price of crude.

Figure 2.5 shows distributions generated from different sets of data. The interesting feature of this graph is that it shows that in some instances locomotives have been nearly worthless at the end of the lease (public data distribution). As valuable as it is to have more information, it does make the decision about locomotive values

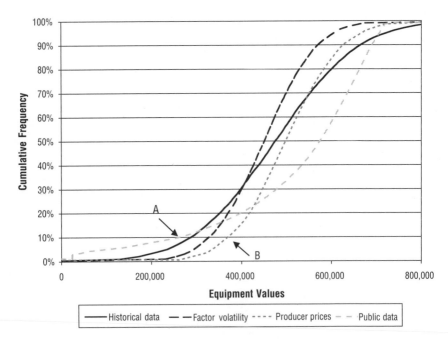

FIGURE 2.5   Multiple Distributions of Equipment Values

more difficult. If you are comfortable with the possibility of missing the estimate 10 percent of the time, there is now a range of values— from $260,000 (point A) to $370,000 (point B). Your decision is based on your confidence in the data sources. Using more information adds to the quality of the decision.

Extreme Events

Distributions should take into account the possibility of extreme events and regime changes. Examples of regime changes are a shift from fixed to floating rates in the foreign exchange market; the sudden one-to-one relationship between prices of Russian bonds and U.S. mortgage-backed securities that occurred in 1998; and the rapid fall in the values of aircraft in 2002. Chapter 3 gives a fuller explanation of regime change and how to implement it when making estimates of future values.

Frequency of Purchase at Lease End

Estimates of equipment values should account for the degree to which lessees purchase the equipment they have been using. It is expected, *a priori*, that where lessee purchase is the norm, volatility will be lower. The information would come from three sources:

1. Historical data of the lessor.
2. Consideration of the industry, equipment leased, and the rate of change of the technology embedded in the equipment.
3. More generally, distributions may be generated from a set of end-of-lease behaviors—purchase of equipment, return of equipment, renewal month-to-month, renewal for a fixed term. The numbers would come from the historical data of the leasing company on the percentage of customers following each behavior and the income from renewal rents and eventual sale.

BASES FOR MEASURING EQUIPMENT RISK

There are three yardsticks for measuring risk—the booked residual in the transaction; the estimated fair market value at the time of the risk measurement; and the historical average (sales price as a percentage of original equipment cost) that has been achieved through sale at the end of the lease.

1. *Booked residual.* The booked residual is the end-of-lease equipment value you estimated when you priced and booked the lease. From an accounting perspective, income has been booked during the life of the lease on the assumption that this value will be realized. Any deviation from the booked value represents a risk.
2. *Fair market value.* The fair market value is an estimate of the equipment value at some future time. It is not a point value but a range of values; hence it does not make an ideal basis for measuring risk.
3. *Historical sales.* The yardstick is the average of historical sales of a particular type of equipment. From an economic perspective this measure is well founded. The shareholders have come to expect a certain equipment value (as a percentage of original cost); therefore, risk is reckoned against this measure.

ESTIMATING FUTURE EQUIPMENT VALUES

There are a number of methods of estimating future equipment values. In this section we'll look at four valuation models—decay curve and volatility; statistical; behavioral; and factor. The choice of a model depends on the information available. The principle in each model is to take into account all of the factors that can be quantified in a systematic and consistent way. The benefits of using the same model for similar types of equipment are that it provides the basis for comparing estimates of the same piece of equipment at different times; it focuses on underlying factors affecting value; and it creates a disciplined approach to forecasting. The results of the model do not provide the final decision; the decision comes by incorporating model results with the factors that cannot be quantified.

Decay Curve and Volatility Valuation Model

This method of estimating future equipment values uses a decay curve and volatility around that curve drawn from historical series of similar prices or factors influencing the price of the equipment.

Many forecasts of equipment values start out with an expected value called a decay curve, or fair market value curve. This curve, which does not include inflation, traces out the value of the equipment over the term of the lease. The decay curve incorporates normal wear and tear, expected future supply and demand for the equipment, and technological change. These curves are often supplied by appraisers or equipment manufacturers, or based on the experience of the lessor's equipment group. Figure 2.6 shows the shape of a typical curve. This is what the decay curve looks like for the Mack trucks you have on lease to R&J Contractors.

The original equipment cost and the decay curve give you point estimates of the equipment value in each year. They are average values, but you know instinctively that the chances of hitting the average every year are small. The next step is to incorporate volatility

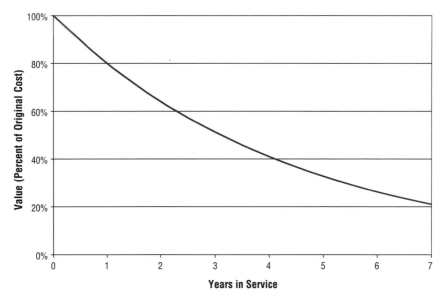

FIGURE 2.6 Decay Curve for Trucks

around the decay curve values. It is assumed that you do not have a historical series of used truck prices available, else you would use them in the analysis.

One source for volatility is the producer price index series for heavy trucks. Producer price indices for new equipment are reasonable proxies of price changes of used equipment. Assuming the new and used equipment do the same job, the used equipment would be readily substitutable for new, and would therefore follow the price index. And since the trucks in your portfolio are used for construction projects, you look at the volatility of construction of highways and roads, adjusted for inflation. Figures 2.7 and 2.8 show the volatility of highway construction and the producer price index for trucks.[1] Also indicated are the 25th, 50th and 75th percentiles. At the 25th percentile, one-quarter of the series are below that number and three-quarters are above it; at the 50th percentile, one-half of the series are below that number and one-half are above it; and so on. The percentiles will be used in

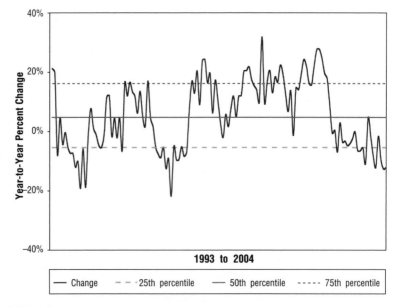

FIGURE 2.7 Volatility of Highway Construction—Adjusted for Inflation
Source: U.S. Census Bureau.

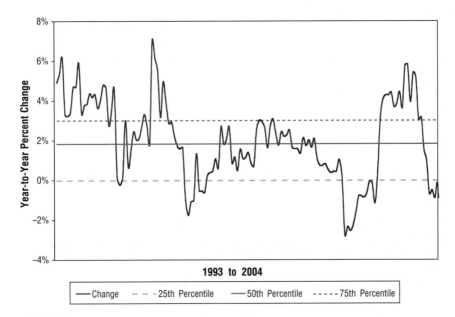

FIGURE 2.8 Volatility of New Truck Price Index
Source: U.S. Department of Labor, Bureau of Labor Statistics.

the next step of the estimation. Highway construction is clearly more variable than the new truck price index, with a range of plus 30 percent to minus 20 percent compared to a range of plus 7 percent to minus 3 percent.

The next step in the evaluation process is to marry the point estimates with the volatility. You want the ability to shape the distribution according to the data rather than use a predefined distribution, such as a normal or lognormal distribution. The Myerson distribution[2] allows you to set lower and upper boundaries beyond which the equipment value estimate will not go; this feature is optional. It also allows you to specify the 25th, 50th, and 75th percentiles in the distribution. The value of the ability to set these parameters is clear from Figure 2.8, where the 25th percentile is nearly two times the distance from the 50th percentile compared to the 75th. In contrast, a normal distribution would constrain the distance to be equal on each side of the 50th percentile.

Given the decay curve and a way of estimating the volatility around it, the next step is to link the estimate in a given year to the estimate in the previous years. This approach defines the average equipment value (50th percentile) for a given year in the following four steps:

1. Start with the equipment value estimated last year.
2. Move last year's estimate closer to the decay curve. This reflects the observed phenomenon that large movements away from the median value—in our case, the decay curve—are likely to be followed by smaller movements. The term for this is *reversion to the mean*. Reversion to the mean is the statistical phenomenon stating that the greater the deviation of a random variable from its median, the greater the probability that the next measured variable will deviate less. The mean reversion suggested by equation 2.1 is a simple one—it takes a fraction of the difference between last year's estimate and the value on the decay curve for last year. A mean reversion adjustment of 0 or a very low percentage is tantamount to starting with last year's value. Another approach would be to let the amount of reversion increase as the difference increased.
3. Adjust for physical wear and tear indicated by the decay curve. This becomes the starting point for this year's estimate.
4. Estimate this year's value, using a Monte Carlo simulation. The idea of Monte Carlo simulation is simple. To look a range of equipment values, 100,000 different paths are generated within the guidelines specified by the boundaries and the percentiles. When a value is chosen for year 3, one-quarter of the time it will fall between the lower boundary of $2,500,000 and the 25th percentile of $4,000,000; one-quarter of the time it will fall between the 75th percentile of $5,800,000 and the upper boundary of $7,000,000; and so on. Figure 2.9 shows but one of the 100,000 possible paths. It took less than 90 seconds to run the simulation.[3]

Figure 2.10 summarizes the distribution of estimated truck values for the last year of the lease. The dashed line is the average, but two-thirds of the occurrences are below the average. The average does not make a very good measure for estimating equipment

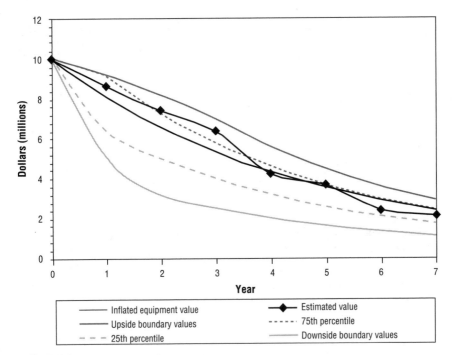

FIGURE 2.9   Equipment Values over Time

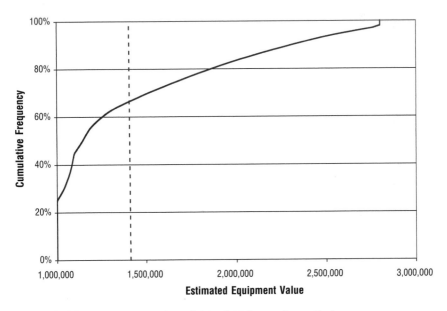

FIGURE 2.10   Distribution of Mack Truck Values at Lease End

values.[4] The entire distribution needs to be considered in making a decision about the amount of the equipment residual to book and on which to base your return calculations.

The formula for the starting point of the equipment value estimate in a given year, e_1, is

$$e_1 = e_0 + (D_0 - e_0) \times R - (D_0 - D_1) \tag{2.1}$$

where e_0 = equipment value in the previous year
 D_0 = decay curve value in the previous year
 R = reversion factor, which can range from 0 (none) to 1 (total reversion)
 D_1 = decay curve value in the current year

As an example, in year 2, if e_0 = \$4,400,000 and D_0 = \$6,000,000, in year 3, if D_1 = \$5,000,000, and R = 0.5, then the starting point for year 3, e_1, is \$4,200,000.

Adding back inflation is straightforward. The inflated equipment value E_1, is

$$E_1 = e_1 \times I^{\wedge t} \tag{2.2}$$

where I = inflation rate
 t = the elapsed number of years from the start of the lease

If you add inflation back in, you may want to adjust the levels of the upper and lower boundaries to reflect it. The equation for generating a distribution of values takes into account the boundary conditions and the 25th and 75th percentiles. A straightforward way of formulating the model is to express the 25th and 75th percentiles and the lower and upper boundaries as percentages of the decay curve, the 50th percentile.[5]

Statistical Valuation Model

This method of estimating future equipment values uses your historical data on sales prices at the end of the lease or data from outside sources such as auctioneers, appraisers, or industry specialists. The basic data required are:

- Equipment types.
- Manufacturer names.
- Model names and numbers.
- Extra features, which increase the original cost of the equipment as well as the sales price relative to equipment without them.
- Year of manufacture.
- Original equipment cost.
- Year of sale.
- Sales price.
- To whom it was sold—the price of the same equipment will be different and the net amount to the lessor will be different depending on whether the equipment is sold to the lessee, to a broker, or at auction.
- Producer price index—as a baseline for estimating future equipment values, the original cost and the sales price should be in constant dollars. Producer price indices for a large number of equipment types are available from the Bureau of Labor Statistics[6] and can be used to put the costs and prices on the same basis.

With this data in hand, you can sort through past experience quickly by applying some simple statistical procedures. In the example that follows, percentiles and lowest and highest sales prices are calculated from the data. You can easily calculate other statistical measures.

This example starts with 900 pieces of information on farm combines. The combines were made between 1989 and 2002 and sold between 1996 and 2002. In 1989 they cost $98,000; in 2002 they cost $153,000.[7] The sales and cost prices are adjusted by the price index for machinery so the effects of inflation are eliminated.

The following figures illustrate the kind of information that can be drawn out of historical data. Figure 2.11, on page 34, shows a historically derived decay curve (the black line) and the distribution around it. All manufacturing years and sales years are included. Notably,

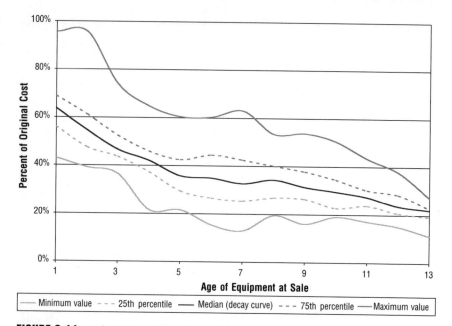

FIGURE 2.11 Sales Prices of Used Combines as They Age
The data in this analysis is used with permission of F.A.C.T.'s Report. © F.A.C.T.'s
Report 2005, www.machinerypete.com.

there is greater volatility around the decay curve at the beginning
and middle of the period than at the end.

Figure 2.12 illustrates the sales experience in different years. The
years 1996, 1997, and 1998 were particularly good years to sell a
used combine. One reason: U.S. wheat production was high in those
years. In forecasting future combine values you want to be mindful
of the fact that these three years are included in your basis of your
forecast. Not that wheat production may not again attain the same
levels, but you may not want to make this assumption the basis of
estimating future equipment values.[8]

The results of this historical analysis are fed into the evaluation model discussed in the previous section to produce a distribution of future combine values. Figure 2.13, on page 36, shows
what the results look like for a lease of six combines with an original equipment cost of $1,000,000, at the end of seven years. On
the basis of historical data, if you were willing to take a 10 percent

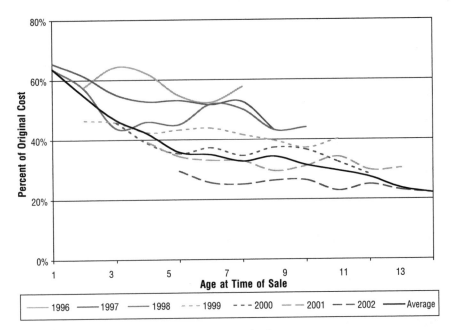

FIGURE 2.12 Age at Time of Sale and Year of Sale
The data in this analysis is used with permission of F.A.C.T.'s Report. © F.A.C.T.'s
Report 2005, www.machinerypete.com.

chance of overestimating the value, you would set the residual at
point A, $159,000; a 20 percent chance leads to a point B value of
$230,000.

Behavioral Valuation Model[9]

The third way of estimating future equipment values and the risk of
owning equipment uses sale prices, but also uses lessee behavior at
the end of the lease. At the end of the initial lease term, some equipment is returned; some equipment is purchased by the lessee; and
the leases on a certain percentage of the equipment are renewed, either month to month or for a fixed period.

At the end of the first renewal period, some equipment is
returned; some equipment is purchased by the lessee; and the leases
on a certain percentage of the equipment are renewed *again*, either
month to month or for a fixed period. And so on . . .

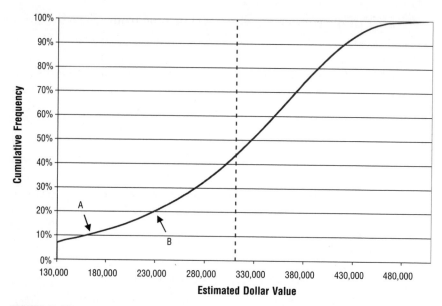

FIGURE 2.13 Estimated Combine Value at the End of Seven Years

A number of lessors track the behavior, the sales price if purchased, the sales price if returned and sold in the market, the lease rates for month-to-month leases, and the rates for fixed-term leases. Re-leasing on a month-to-month basis or for a fixed term at the end of a lease, prior to the eventual sale of the equipment, adds value to the equipment and tends to reduce equipment risk.

This behavioral information is married with some statistical techniques to estimate future equipment values and risk. The initial inputs into the evaluation model are

- Probability of each outcome.
- The distribution around the probability of the outcome.
- Income from each outcome.
- The distribution around the income.
- The number of month-to-month renewals.
- Tenor of fixed-term renewals.
- Discount rate, to sum up the values at the end of the initial lease.

After the end of the initial lease, four subsequent periods are tracked. The income to each outcome includes both the ultimate sales price of the equipment and rental income from renewals. Table 2.1, on pages 38 and 39, illustrates how the behavioral evaluation model is set up.

In order to illustrate the behavioral nature of the model, some simple distribution assumptions are used. The number of data points, or sample size, determines the width of the distribution around the probabilities of each outcome. The distribution is wider when fewer data points are available, to reflect the uncertainty of how representative the data are. This is the meaning of the selection box in the top right corner of the figure. The type of equipment determines the distribution around the ultimate rent and sale numbers; for example, the volatility is higher, so the distribution is wider, for computer equipment than for forklifts. Clearly, the distribution assumptions can be specified more precisely.

The output of the behavioral evaluation model is generated by Monte Carlo simulation and the results are similar to those shown for the previous evaluation models. Figure 2.14, on page 40, is a typical outcome of the model. Even though the input distributions are wide (reflecting high volatility), the output of the behavioral model shows a relatively tight range of outcomes. About 85 percent of the estimated values are clustered, plus or minus $5,000 of the average. Knowledge of lessee behavior at lease end, and your ability to track it, reduces the amount of equipment risk you have at lease end.

The six steps for going from the inputs to the outputs are:

1. For each period, specify the distributions around the probabilities of the four outcomes—return, sale to lessee, lease renewal month-to-month, or lease renewal fixed-term.
2. Constrain the sum of the probabilities to be 100 percent. Even if the average probabilities equal 100 percent, it is not necessarily true that when numbers are chosen from each distribution they too will add to 100 percent, hence the constraint.
3. Calculate the renewal, purchase, and return probabilities in each period. For example, at lease end, 40 percent of the lessees renew on a month-to-month basis. At lease end plus 1, of that 40 percent, 30 percent will return the equipment, 40 percent will renew again on a month-to-month basis, 10 percent will renew on a term basis, and 20 percent will purchase

TABLE 2.1 Behavioral Valuation Model

Outcome Probabilities

End-of-Lease Outcomes	Lease End Probability	Lease End Term of Renewal (Months)	Lease End + 1 Probability	Lease End + 1 Term of Renewal (Months)	Lease End + 2 Probability	Lease End + 2 Term of Renewal (Months)	Lease End + 3 Probability	Lease End + 3 Term of Renewal (Months)	Final Disposition Probability	Small or Concentrated Sample
Return	15%		30%		45%		50%		70%	Yes ○
Renew month-to-month	40	4	40	4	20	4	20	4		
Renew fixed-term	20	12	10	12	15	12	10	12		No ●
Purchase	25		20		20		20		30	

Sales Prices

End-of-Lease Outcomes	Lease End Sale	Lease End + 1 Rent and Sale Mo. to Mo.	Lease End + 1 Rent and Sale Fixed	Lease End + 2 Rent and Sale Mo. to Mo.	Lease End + 2 Rent and Sale Fixed	Lease End + 3 Rent and Sale Mo. to Mo.	Lease End + 3 Rent and Sale Fixed	Final Disposition Rent and Sale Mo. to Mo.	Final Disposition Rent and Sale Fixed
Return	$ 4	$ 8	$ 8	$20	$12	$28	$16	$36	$18
Purchase	31	33	33	36	35	38	38	40	40

Rent and Sale Volatility

	Lease End	Lease End + 1	Lease End + 2	Lease End + 3	Final Disposition
High	●	●	●	●	●
Low	○	○	○	○	○

Discount Rates

	Lease End	Lease End + 1		Lease End + 2		Lease End + 3		Final Disposition	
		Mo. to Mo.	Fixed	Mo. to Mo.	Fixed	Mo. to Mo.	Fixed	Mo. to Mo.	Fixed
		1.10%	1.90%	1.50%	2.20%	1.90%	2.40%	2.00%	2.70%

Values Discounted to Lease End

	Lease End	Lease End + 1	Lease End + 2	Lease End + 3	Final Disposition
Return	$ 0.17	$2.00	$2.52	$1.31	$0.75
Purchase	11.87	8.76	2.87	0.41	0.31

Outcome

Value of residual	$30.97

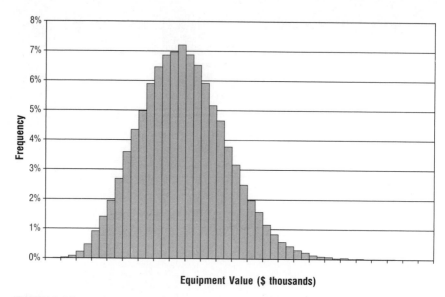

Equipment Value ($ thousands)

FIGURE 2.14 Distribution of End of Lease Equipment Values

the equipment. This means that going toward the next period, out of the original population of lessees, 12 percent (40 percent × 30 percent) will return the equipment, 16 percent (40 percent × 40 percent) will renew month-to-month, 4 percent will renew on a term basis, and 20 percent of the lessees will purchase the equipment.

4. For each period, specify the distributions around the rent and sales numbers.
5. Multiply the renewal, purchase, and return numbers (step 3) by the rent and sales numbers (step 4).
6. Sum up the results in each period and discount them back to lease end.

Factor Valuation Model

The fourth method of estimating future equipment values establishes a relationship between the historical price of a piece of equipment and relevant economic factors. This is particularly useful when making long-term forecasts—for example, an airplane or locomotive 20 to 25 years in the future. Once the relationship is established, you have access to a wider body of knowledge about basic economic variables such as gross domestic product, interest rates, and oil prices; there are more experts with reasoned views on these topics than on the price of a locomotive.

The first step is to identify the economic factors most pertinent to the equipment in your portfolio. Regression analysis is used to establish the relationship between equipment prices and the factors. The prototype is an equation like

$$y = a + b_1 x_1 + b_2 x_2 + b_3 x_3 + u \qquad (2.3)$$

where y = price of the airplane
x = macroeconomic factors
b = regression coefficients
a = a constant
u = value not explained by the macro economic variables.[10]

The second step is to develop a process that simulates the movement of the macroeconomic factors. As an example, the movement of short-term interest rates follows a random process with the following characteristics: The average rate in any one year is no more than 30 percent different from the previous year, but having hit the boundary it tends to revert to its long-term average. Econometricians have developed many of the processes for macroeconomic factors. Some research in economic journals is required to determine those that provide the best time-tested results for particular factors.

The third step is to use a Monte Carlo program to simulate the macroeconomic factors, the x's, within the regression equations. This will produce a distribution of equipment prices for future periods.

These three steps would be performed for each equipment class every 18 months, or when you believe a sea change has occurred in the relation between macroeconomic factors and equipment prices.

DATA

Lessors often claim that they have insufficient data from which to draw any conclusions or that there is a story behind each data point that makes it noncomparable to the next, so they conclude that they are unable to use statistical methods to estimate equipment values. But increasingly, statisticians are using the bootstrap method[11] to validate the inferences they draw from small data sets. The method is well established in statistics and is often used in medical trials.

The purpose of the bootstrap method is to determine if the statistics, such as the average, the standard deviation, or the 75th percentile, that are calculated from a sample of the population would be the same if they were calculated from the entire population.

With the bootstrap method, the sample is treated as the population and a Monte Carlo style procedure is conducted on it. The procedure randomly draws a large number of resamples from the original sample, replacing each element after it is drawn. Each resample will have the same number of elements as the original; it can include some of the original data elements more than once, and some are not included. From each resample the desired calculations—mean, standard deviation, and percentiles—are made. From 1,000 resamples you have a distribution of means, standard deviations, and percentiles. The percentiles and standard deviations chosen to make the estimates of future equipment values are those in which you have a high degree of confidence, say at the 90 or 95 percent level.[12]

APPENDIX—DISTRIBUTIONS

A distribution of values can be looked at a number of different ways. The following figures illustrate the three most popular ways of displaying distributions. In all of the graphs, the future values are on the horizontal axis and their frequency is on the vertical axis. *Frequency* means the percentage of times a particular value is expected to occur. We also speak of the probability, chance or likelihood of occurrence. In Figure 2.15 the values were divided up into bins of two numbers; for a range of 100 there are 50 bins. The histogram depicts the probability a future value will occur. The height of the bar represents the probability. For example, there is a 7.5 percent probability the future value will be in the 51–53 bin. The sum of all of the bars is 100 percent.

Figure 2.16, on page 44, is called a frequency distribution and it tells a similar story. The height of the line indicates the probability that a certain value will occur. For example, there is a probability of 15 percent that the future value will be 38. Again, the sum of all of the probabilities under the curve is 100 percent.

The third representation is the cumulative frequency distribution, Figure 2.17, on page 44. The cumulative graph shows the probability that a future value is less than or equal to any particular number. For example, the probability that the future value is less than or equal to 40 is 16 percent (point A), while the probability that the future value is less than or equal to 60 is 84 percent (point B). It is now more apparent that the probabilities sum to 100 percent. The cumulative frequency distribution is

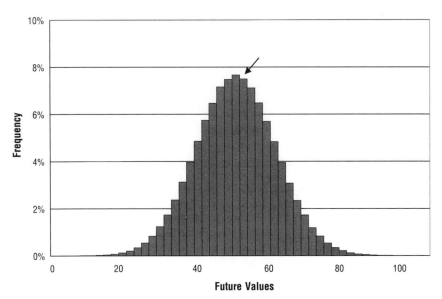

FIGURE 2.15 Histogram

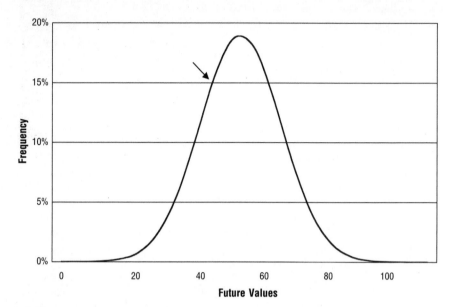

FIGURE 2.16 Frequency Distribution

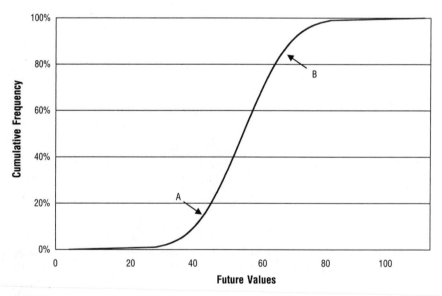

FIGURE 2.17 Cumulative Frequency Distribution

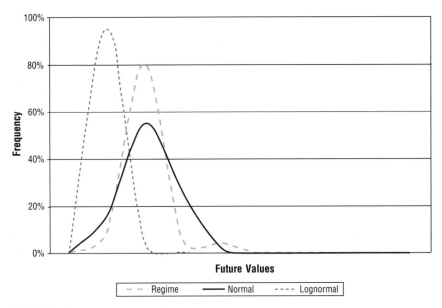

FIGURE 2.18 Types of Distributions

somewhat easier to use when expressing the likelihood of a future value. It literally sums up the frequency distribution shown in Figure 2.16.

Distribution curves are also characterized by their shape. The classic bell-shaped curve shown in Figure 2.16 is described as normal. Other distributions are generally classified with reference to the normal curve. Figure 2.18 shows examples of a number of different distributions. The reasons for the different distributions are that the underlying data in the world, when assembled, produces different shapes, or we think it should.

The lognormal distribution is characterized by being skewed to one side, either to the left or to the right. It is used in the instances where there is the possibility of one-off significant events happening. For example, when thinking about large corporate credit defaults, there are generally few, but when they happen they are large. The regime distribution is a weighted combination of two normal distributions with different averages. It is used to represent situations where there is a shift in the way the world works. For example, prior to 1990, San Francisco commercial rents increased about 5 percent a year; in the mid to late 1990s they increased about 25 percent a year. A single distribution will not capture those phenomena, so a distribution is constructed to include a shift from one state of the world (regime) to another.

CHAPTER 3

Credit Risk

In Chapter 1, Figures 1.1 and 1.3 show the importance of rent to the lessor. Credit risk is the uncertainty about whether the lessee will make the remaining rent payments. However, the credit risk of leases is different than for most other financial instruments.

- The term is longer. Leases on rail cars, locomotives, airplanes, and power plants typically last at least 15 years and sometimes 30 years. (Home mortgages are often 30 years, but most do not last more than five or six years because home owners refinance or move.)
- The risk changes over time. Credit risk changes because the amount owed the lessor changes.
- The risk is different from lease to lease. In a leveraged lease the amount at risk goes up before falling.
- The way the rent stream is structured—front-loaded, back-loaded, or level rent payments—affects the risk. In addition, in a leveraged lease the amount at risk is governed by the way rent payments are allocated between the lender and the lessor in each structure.

These points are illustrated in Figure 3.1 on page 48. It shows the amount at risk on two leveraged rail car leases. On the horizontal axis are the elapsed years of the lease and on the vertical axis are the amounts at risk. In lease 1 the lender, not the lessor, receives most of the rent for most of the lease. In lease 2 the lessor structures the allocation of the rent payments to keep the amount at risk below its initial investment.

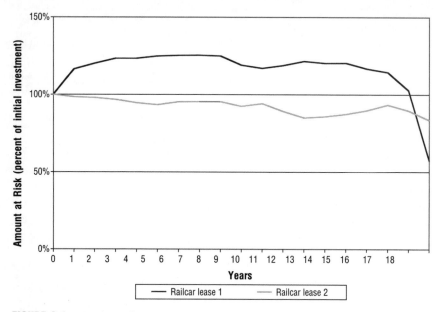

FIGURE 3.1   Credit Risk over Time—Leveraged Leases

To estimate and model credit risk you need four pieces of information:

1. *Probability of default*—the probability that a lessee will default on rent payments.
2. *Migration*—the way that probability changes as time goes on.
3. *Recovery*—how much you will recover if the lessee defaults.
4. The *volatility* of the previous three events.

PROBABILITY OF DEFAULT

There are a number of approaches to estimating the probability that a lessee will default—from historical data, from models, or as a function of business cycles. The reason for reviewing the different approaches is to choose those elements that are most relevant to the credit risk of leases.

Historical Data

Moody's Investors Service and Standard & Poor's publish historical series on default rates. The information is broken down by year and by the credit rating and industry of the lessee.[1] Table 3.1, on page 50, is an example of the data published by Moody's, broken down by credit rating of the companies.[2] It shows the default rates of companies of a given credit rating over time. The table is built up by looking at the ratings of companies in year 1, say starting in 1970, and then following those companies for the next 20 years to see how they perform.[3] For example, of the companies rated Ba in the first year, 1.22 percent defaulted in that year; one year later a total of 3.34 percent defaulted; and by the end of the third year a total of 5.97 percent defaulted. When the companies defaulted they were not necessarily rated Ba, but they had been at the start. This table averages such experience using each of the 35 years from 1970 to 2004 as the starting years. These series provide you with a basis to estimate the creditworthiness of lessees over long periods of time.

From the cumulative default rates you can figure out the probability of default in some future year assuming the lessee has survived until that time. The equation for the forward default probability in any year in the future is:

$$DR(t + 1 | t) = \frac{DR_{t+1} - DR_t}{1 - DR_t} \qquad (3.1)$$

where DR_{t+1} = cumulative default rate in any year
DR_t = cumulative default rate in the year before

For example, for a Baa rated company in year 7, the forward rate is 0.54 percent.

Figures 3.2 and 3.3, on page 51, are charts of the forward default rates. Investment grade and sub–investment grade ratings are on two different charts because of the difference in scale. All of the investment grade ratings are below 1 percent; the sub–investment grade ratings start at 1 percent and go up from there. The default rates for investment grades tend to rise over time; those for sub–investment grades tend to fall.

TABLE 3.1 Cumulative Default Rates (percent)

Average Issuer-Weighted Cumulative Default Rates by Whole Letter Rating, 1970–2004

Cohort Rating	Time Horizon (Years)																			
	1	2	3	4	5	6	7	8	9	10	11	12	13	14	15	16	17	18	19	20
Aaa	0	0	0	0.04	0.12	0.21	0.3	0.41	0.52	0.63	0.76	0.9	1.05	1.13	1.22	1.32	1.42	1.54	1.54	1.54
Aa	0	0.03	0.03	0.12	0.2	0.29	0.37	0.47	0.54	0.61	0.69	0.84	1.01	1.25	1.38	1.52	1.73	1.92	2.2	2.44
A	0.02	0.08	0.22	0.36	0.5	0.67	0.85	1.04	1.25	1.48	1.72	1.95	2.2	2.43	2.74	3.12	3.51	3.93	4.41	4.87
Baa	0.19	0.54	0.98	1.55	2.08	2.59	3.12	3.65	4.25	4.89	5.59	6.35	7.12	7.91	8.73	9.48	10.23	10.94	11.56	12.05
Ba	1.22	3.34	5.79	8.27	10.72	12.98	14.81	16.64	18.4	20.11	22.01	24.07	26.11	28.02	29.67	31.53	33.16	34.71	35.92	37.07
B	5.81	12.93	19.51	25.33	30.48	35.1	39.45	42.89	45.89	48.64	50.99	52.85	54.62	56.35	57.72	58.8	59.11	59.11	59.11	59.11
Caa-C	22.43	35.96	46.71	54.19	59.72	64.49	68.06	71.91	74.53	76.77	78.53	78.53	78.53	78.53	78.53	78.53	78.53	78.53	78.53	78.53
IG	0.07	0.21	0.41	0.67	0.92	1.17	1.44	1.7	1.99	2.31	2.64	3.01	3.39	3.77	4.18	4.61	5.04	5.48	5.92	6.31
SG	4.85	9.84	14.43	18.41	21.91	24.95	27.52	29.76	31.75	33.61	35.47	37.27	39.05	40.71	42.13	43.65	44.87	46	46.89	47.75
All Rated	1.56	3.15	4.6	5.86	6.94	7.85	8.62	9.3	9.93	10.53	11.14	11.75	12.37	12.95	13.51	14.1	14.65	15.18	15.68	16.13

IG indicates investment grade, SG indicates sub-investment grade.

Source: Moody's Investors Service.

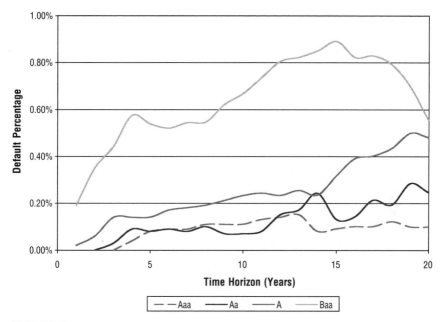

FIGURE 3.2   Forward Default Rates for Investment Grade Ratings

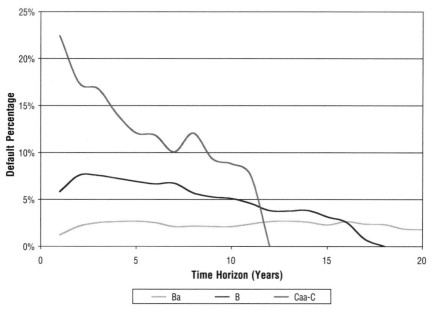

FIGURE 3.3   Forward Default Rates for Sub–Investment Grade Ratings

In Figure 3.3, on page 51, the forward default rate for Caa-C rated companies is zero after 11 years and the forward default rate for B rated companies is zero after 17 years. The companies that initially had that rating have either fallen (most of them) or achieved a higher rating.

In addition to the average forward default rates, you need to know how volatile they are. Figure 3.4 shows the parameters for Ba rated companies. At least 75 percent of the time the default rate in any year does not go over 4 percent, but 25 percent of the time it does, with significant consequences to a lessor.

Historical data shows how lessees may behave, in terms of the trend and the volatility around it as they age. This time perspective is particularly important for long-term leases.

Models

The four principal models, outside proprietary ones, used by financial institutions to estimate the probability of default are Credit Monitor, CreditMetrics, CreditRisk+, and Kamakura Risk Manager.[4] The models focus on more than the probability of default; they include

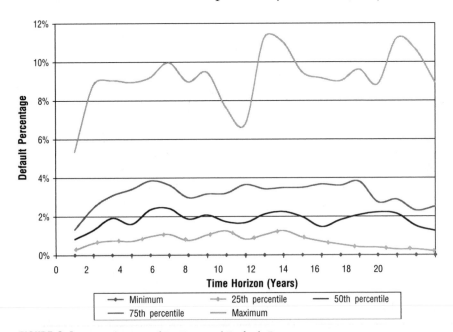

FIGURE 3.4 Distribution of Ba Forward Default Rates

migration of credit risk, recovery, and the portfolio aspects of credit risk. In this section only the probability of default aspect of the models is considered.

Credit Monitor combines information from financial statements with investors' views and forecasts of a lessee, as embodied in its stock price, to estimate the probability of default. It compares the market value of a lessee's assets to its contractual liabilities. Considering the nature of the liabilities and historical experience, a default point is chosen for each lessee. The market value of a lessee's assets is derived from the price of its stock. The lower the stock price, the lower the market value of the assets. The volatility of the stock price produces a series of asset values. As the market value of the assets becomes close to the value of the contractual liabilities, the likelihood of default increases.[5] Figure 3.5 is an illustration of the process.[6]

CreditMetrics approaches credit risk from a different point of view. The model starts with the current rating of a lessee, say a Moody's rating of Ba, then looks at where and with what

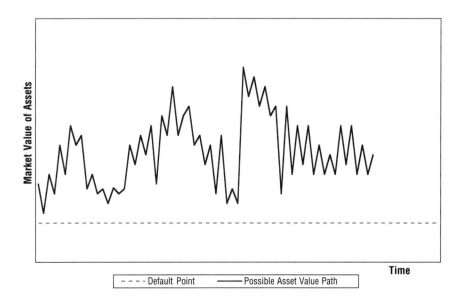

FIGURE 3.5 KMV Default Probability
Source: Peter J. Crosbie and Jeffrey R. Bohn, *Modeling Default Risk* (San Francisco: KMV, 2002).

probability the lessee will remain a Ba, or migrate downward, or upward.[7]

CreditRisk+ works by allocating a default rate to a lessee. The default rate can be derived either from the credit spread on the company's bond or from the lessor's own store of historical information, or obtained from rating agency statistics. In addition, the model incorporates default rate volatility to reflect the phenomena shown in Figure 3.4 on page 52. The effect of adding volatility in the CreditRisk+ model is to increase the number of losses at the tail of the loss distribution without changing the average number of losses. The lognormal curve in Figure 2.19, on page 45, is an example. If the horizontal axis is relabeled losses, you see there are more losses in the right-hand tail of the distribution, compared to the normal distribution, though they have the same average and standard deviation.[8]

Kamakura's model uses return on assets, leverage, relative stock performance, stock price volatility, interest rates, other macro variables like oil prices, and company size and industry. The model incorporates data from more sources—the company, the market, and the economy—than other models. The default probability is modeled as a hazard rate, which can be interpreted as the ratio of the probability of default (PD) and the probability of surviving (1 − PD). It would be written PD/(1 − PD).

A shock term $Z(t)$ is used to create random movements in the macro factors (like oil prices) linked to a specific company. The macro factors in turn drive the default probability. Changes in macro factors link them to changes in interest rates and random shocks.

$$\Delta M_t = M_t \times [r_t \Delta t + \sigma_m \times \Delta Z_t] \qquad (3.2)$$

where ΔM_t = change in macro factors

M_t = series of macro factors

$r_t \Delta t$ = random interest rate

ΔZ_t = changes in the shock term

σ_m = volatility of the macro factor[9]

Business Cycles

There is not a clear consensus on the relationship between the state of the economy and credit risk. The different views can be illustrated by considering two stylized cyclical patterns. In the first, the business cycle is described by a sine wave. A boom will be followed by a recession and a recession by a recovery. The associated default probability model shows an increase in credit risk around the peak of the business cycle, given the imminent recession, and a reduction in credit risk around the trough of the cycle, given the imminent recovery. The second view is that business cycles are so irregular that the economy's current state is the best indicator of the future. A boom does not mean that a recession is imminent and a recession does not mean that a recovery is likely. The default probability model associated with this view shows a decline in credit risk when economic conditions are strong—on the basis that the strong conditions are likely to continue—and an increase in credit risk when economic conditions are depressed.

A third, and more tenable, view is that risk is built up in a boom and materializes in a downturn. The forces that drive economic expansions often sow the seeds of future recessions by generating imbalances in the financial system or the real economy. Such imbalances arise from rapid and sustained growth in credit or asset prices (stocks or housing). When the imbalances are righted, the process poses considerable costs to the economy and increases the probability of default. Accordingly, while these imbalances cannot be measured perfectly, they can be measured beforehand. This logic suggests that periods of very strong economic growth might be followed by an above average level of credit risk.[10]

Observations

Models that incorporate business cycles are useful for lessors because of the long-term nature of many leases. In a 10-year lease, a lessee may be subject to as many as three different cycles. Estimating the exact timing of the cycles is less important than recognizing that during the term of the lease it is prudent to subject the lessee's paying ability to cyclical movements. Assessing credit risk means making an informed judgment about how the lessee will fare during downturns and its ability to replenish reserves in an upturn.

There are two main difficulties with models that rely heavily on markets to drive their results. Credit Monitor relies exclusively on the stock market to drive its results; the Kamakura model does so to a lesser extent. First, stock prices occasionally move away from the fundamental values of the lessee. A ramp up or a fall in the stock price will send overly positive or overly negative signals about the chances of default. Second, because the stock market is volatile, default probabilities may be high one month and low the next, and can move significantly without any change in the fundamentals of the lessee.

MIGRATION

Migration adds the time dimension to probability of default. Migration describes the path the default probability may follow over the life of a lease. Is the lessee becoming more likely or less likely to default? As noted, the amount at risk changes over time in a lease. Equally important, what is happening to the creditworthiness of the lessee? Migration has been alluded to in discussing the different approaches to probability of default.

Table 3.2, on pages 57 and 58, is taken from Moody's default study by Hamilton.[11] It shows the movement of companies' credit ratings over three different periods—1 year, 5 years, and 10 years. The migration tables are calculated from 35 years of history. The number of companies remaining in the same rating category decreases dramatically over time. Look at Ba: After 1 year 78.88 percent are still Ba; after 5 years, 32.12 percent are Ba; after 10 years, only 11.30 percent. The most notable observation on the tables is that nearly all of the movement is downward—toward higher default probabilities. The only exception is the Baa category; over 5 and 10 years these companies tend to improve their creditworthiness.

One of the aspects of migration that is not apparent from Table 3.2 is the momentum of rating changes. Moody's reports that companies that undergo rating change in one year are much more likely to have change in the same direction in the following year, compared to companies that have no rating change, or to reverse their

TABLE 3.2 Ratings Migration Tables

Average 1-Year Whole Letter Rating Migration Matrix, 1970–2004

Initial Rating	Number of Issuers	Aaa	Aa	A	Baa	Ba	B	Caa-C	Default	Rating Withdrawn
Aaa	3,179	89.48	7.05	0.75	0	0.03	0	0	0	2.69
Aa	11,310	1.07	88.41	7.35	0.25	0.07	0.01	0	0	2.83
A	22,981	0.05	2.32	88.97	4.85	0.46	0.12	0.01	0.02	3.19
Baa	18,368	0.05	0.23	5.03	84.5	4.6	0.74	0.15	0.16	4.54
Ba	12,702	0.01	0.04	0.46	5.28	78.88	6.48	0.5	1.16	7.19
B	10,794	0.01	0.03	0.12	0.4	6.18	77.45	2.93	6.03	6.85
Caa-C	2,091	0	0	0	0.52	1.57	4	62.68	23.12	8.11

Average 5-Year Whole Letter Rating Migration Matrix, 1970–2004

Initial Rating	Number of Issuers	Aaa	Aa	A	Baa	Ba	B	Caa-C	Default	Rating Withdrawn
Aaa	2,792	56.88	23.78	5.58	0.46	0.4	0.04	0.08	0.11	12.67
Aa	8,751	4.16	53.86	23.13	3.58	0.9	0.29	0.02	0.21	13.84
A	18,268	0.25	8.15	57.83	14.2	2.95	0.82	0.16	0.43	15.22
Baa	14,116	0.24	1.51	15.64	47.05	9.58	2.65	0.47	1.72	21.14
Ba	10,923	0.08	0.25	2.98	12.53	32.12	11.1	1.07	8.12	31.76
B	7,720	0.05	0.08	0.51	2.82	12.55	29.56	2.31	20.58	31.54
Caa-C	1,073	0	0	0	3.03	5.62	7.06	15.12	42.85	26.31

(Continued)

TABLE 3.2 *(Continued)*

Average 10-Year Whole Letter Rating Migration Matrix, 1970–2004

Initial Rating	Number of Issuers	Terminal Rating								
		Aaa	Aa	A	Baa	Ba	B	Caa-C	Default	Rating Withdrawn
Aaa	2,278	32.38	30.47	10.41	2.97	0.76	0.1	0.05	0.6	22.26
Aa	5,888	4.83	30.2	28.25	7.94	2.32	0.58	0.09	0.78	25.01
A	12,500	0.36	10.4	38.29	15.66	4.32	1.53	0.24	1.24	27.96
Baa	9,830	0.21	2.38	17.33	26.84	7.81	3.08	0.38	3.63	38.35
Ba	7,919	0.2	0.81	5.26	11.37	11.3	6.82	0.7	13.67	49.87
B	3,992	0.06	0.03	1.62	3.98	8.58	9.41	0.75	27.39	48.18
Caa-C	327	0	0	0	4.49	1.92	1.85	2.14	50.42	39.17

The initial rating of the company is in the left-most column. The top row indicates where the lessee ended up after 1, 5, or 10 years. The numbers are percentages of the companies in the category after the elapsed number of years.
Source: Moody's Investors Service.

change.[12] History suggests that when thinking about default probability over time, once a change occurs it is likely to continue for a
period of time. This is in contrast to the concept of mean reversion
used for equipment values.

CreditMetrics uses migration tables in its model to estimate future default probabilities. A reasonable amount of effort is spent to
ensure that the migration tables used in their model are consistent.
The steps taken by CreditMetrics ensure that:

- Rank order is preserved. For example, at the end of 10 years,
  companies rated Aaa have default probabilities lower than companies rated Baa.
- The migration tables are consistent with the cumulative default
  tables, like Table 3.1.
- Rating path behavior is ordered. For example, at the end of
  one year, more Baa rated companies than A rated companies
  become Ba.[13]

However, this search for consistency may be misplaced since research on migration suggests that the chance of moving from one
rating (and its associated default probability) to another rating
changes over time.[14]

Credit Monitor models future default probabilities by using historical asset volatility and by making some assumptions about asset
growth and the company's debt. CreditRisk+ treats default rates in
the future in the same way as the present, coupling a default probability with a distribution around it. Kamakura models the future by
simulating changes in the underlying macro variables that drive the
probability of default.

CONCLUSIONS

The following conclusion relevant to lessee credit risk can be drawn
from the discussion of migration and probability of default:

- Default probabilities tend to increase over time for investment
  grade credit ratings and decrease for sub–investment grades.

- Once a path of increasing or decreasing probabilities is established, the path continues in the same direction for some period.
- The movement along the path is not regular, in timing or in the size of the steps.
- Historical data provides a good basis for making estimates of default probability, especially for long-term leases.
- Macroeconomic factors help to explain the behavior of default probabilities.

DEFAULT AND MIGRATION MODEL

In this section the equations that incorporate the conclusions are developed. The first step is to specify the distribution of the probability of default for a given credit rating in any year.

$$PD_R = M(LB, 25th, 50th, 75th, UB) \qquad (3.3)$$

where PD_R = probability of default for a given credit rating

$M(\ )$ = indicates a Myerson distribution

LB = lower bound of the distribution, a number close to but not zero because zero is equivalent to no default

50th = actual historical 50th percentile

25th, 75th = the average of those percentiles over 20 years. They are modeled to be a constant distance from the changing 50th percentile

UB = upper bound of the distribution, the highest default rate ever experienced by the companies in the specified credit rating

The second step is to specify the movement from one period to the next. The observed momentum in default rates is incorporated in equation (3.4).[15]

$$PD_{Rt} = A \times PD_{t-2} + B \times PD_{t-1} + C \times M(LB, 25\text{th}, 50\text{th}, 75\text{th}, UB)_t \quad (3.4)$$

where PD_{Rt} = probability of default for rating R in year t

          A, B, C = coefficients that weigh the influence of the past and present, summing to 1, and are estimated from the historical data

          $M(\ )$ = Myerson distribution parameters, the same as defined for equation (3.3).

Figures 3.6 and 3.7 show the graphical output of equation (3.4). Figure 3.6 shows five of the 10,000 Monte Carlo simulation trials that are run. The graph demonstrates that equation (3.4) incorporates the conclusions. Only the last, relating to macroeconomic influences, has not been incorporated.

Figure 3.7, on page 62, illustrates the distribution of default probabilities for a given year. Think of it as a cross section of 10,000 of these lines for year 10. The curve displays the characteristics most associated with default probabilities—highly concentrated around the average, but still a significant probability of a high default rate, moving to the right.

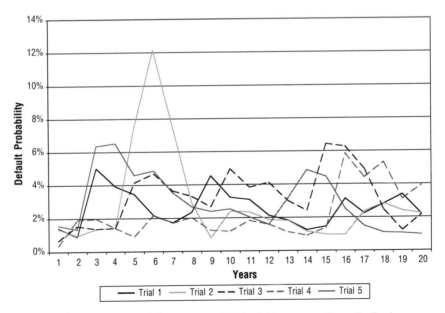

FIGURE 3.6 Simulation of the Pattern of Default Rates over Time, Ba Rating

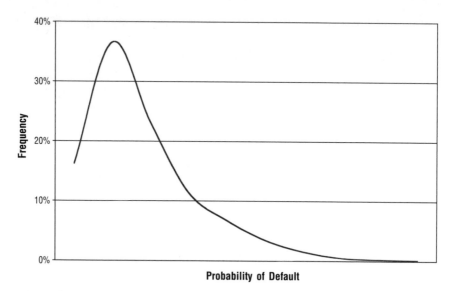

FIGURE 3.7   Distribution of Default Probabilities

REGIMES

Recall that when looking at the probabilities of default, there was a sizeable spread between the 75th percentile and the maximum. There is another way of handling this phenomenon rather than attempting to capture all possibilities in one distribution. One approach is to think about different regimes.[16] There are precedents in finance as well as other fields for thinking about regime changes. A few examples: The dot.com boom and bust created totally different patterns in stock prices, housing prices, and employment; in 1972 the switch from fixed to floating exchange rates created distinctly different patterns of exchange rate movement. There is no reason to believe that an unforeseen event may not occur in the future. In thinking about a Ba rated lessee, the first regime features a default rate that averages roughly 1 percent over 20 years. The second regime features a much higher default rate, 6.7 percent.

There are a number of ways to incorporate different regimes into a model; two of them are considered here. The first way is to link them in terms of the probability of occurrence. The probability can be taken from history or your projection of the future. For example, in the present instance the low default rate regime happens 75 percent of the time and the high default rate regime happens 25 percent of the time. If you use a Monte Carlo simulation to choose randomly from each regime, three-quarters of the time you will choose a probability from somewhere in the low default rate distribution and one-quarter of the time you will choose a probability from somewhere in the high default rate distribution. If you were to use normal distributions to characterize each regime, the equation looks like this:

$$PD = \text{if } I(1, 100) \le 75, \text{ then } N_1(0.011, 0.008),$$
$$\text{else } N_2(0.067, 0.02) \tag{3.5}$$

where PD = probability of default
$I(1, 100)$ = integer function from 1 to 100
$N_1(\ ,\ )$ = normal distribution for the first regime
$N_2(\ ,\ )$ = normal distribution for the second regime

And for an average year the outcomes look like Figure 3.8. The two regimes are evident from the figure with the first peaking around 1 percent and the second around 7 percent.

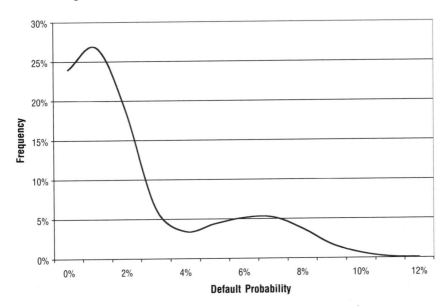

FIGURE 3.8 Distribution of Default Probability with Regime Switching

A second way of incorporating two regimes is to link them to a function containing one or more macro variables such as business credit outstanding or S&P 500 price/earnings ratios. They are good indicators of the buildup of imbalances in the economy that subsequently result in an increase in defaults. Out-of-pattern increases in these variables trigger a shift to the second regime. Equation (3.5), on page 63, can be rewritten to reflect that an increase of either variable, putting it at the far end (say 90th percentile) of its historical distribution, shifts the default probability from the first regime to the second regime two years later. Equation (3.6) is an expression of this function:

$$PD_t = \text{if } (c > \chi, \text{ or } p > \pi)_{t-2} \text{ then } N_2(0.067, 0.02)_t$$
$$\text{else } N_1(0.011, .008)_t \qquad (3.6)$$

where
PD_t = probability of default
c = change in corporate loans outstanding
χ = value of the change in corporate loans outstanding at a specified percentile
p = price/earnings ratio
π = value of the price/earnings ratio at a specified percentile
$N_1(\ ,\ )$ = normal distribution for the first regime
$N_2(\ ,\ )$ = normal distribution for the second regime
t and $t-2$ = time lag of the effect of the variables

This formulation is a way of incorporating macroeconomic factors into default probabilities.

RECOVERY

If a lessee defaults on its lease, how much can you expect to recover? Since you own the equipment, your first concern is how much it is worth when the lessee defaults. In Chapter 2 we looked at how to estimate the future value of equipment. Those equations are combined with equations for estimating the contractual claims the

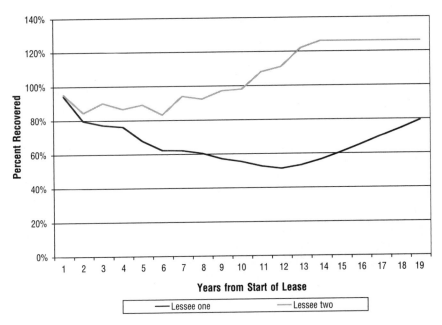

FIGURE 3.9 Recovery

lessor has on the lessee. The two will produce a model for estimating recoveries that is specific to leasing.

The reasons for estimating recoveries are that it tells you how to structure a lease when you first originate it and it tells you the best course of action to pursue if a default occurs. Figure 3.9 shows the difference structuring can make. It shows the estimated recoveries on two different leases. These are actual leases to two different lessees; both are 15-year leases, both have an after-tax yield of 5.6 percent, and the equipment in both leases is box cars. In lease 1 the residual was set at 35 percent and nearly all of the rent goes to the nonrecourse lender until the loan is repaid. In lease 2 the amount of money the lessor puts in the transaction is larger, the residual is set at 20 percent, and the lessor shares the rents with the lender.

Contractual Claims

On the basis of contractual law and the U.S. bankruptcy code, the lessor can make certain claims when a lessee declares bankruptcy. The claims rank as senior unsecured obligations of the lessee.

According to a study by Standard & Poor's, there is little cushion under senior unsecured debt to draw on in bankruptcy. On average it is 15 percent, compared to bank debt with its cushion of about 45 percent. As a result, recoveries for bank debt have historically averaged 83 percent and for senior unsecured bonds averaged 49 percent.[17] Statistics that include 2001 and 2002, however, show that recoveries for senior unsecured bonds fell to an average of 39 percent.[18] The same studies show that there is a very wide distribution around these averages so that any estimating procedure should use a distribution of values rather than a single value. Other variables that affect recoveries are the industry of the defaulting company (less is recovered in an airline default than in the default of a cable TV company) and the location of the company.

There are five different ways to estimate how much you will recover in the event one of your lessees defaults.[19] The following equations show how to calculate the recovery amount for a leveraged lease. For a single investor or operating lease, simply drop the terms relating to loan, principal payments, and accrued interest. The results will be a distribution of values for each scenario because future equipment values, the percentage of the claim you will recover, and the probability that the lease will be reaffirmed are all distributions. You calculate each scenario and then choose the one that has the largest recovery and smallest dispersion around it. This is the one you would choose in a workout situation and to estimate your recovery.

Sell the Equipment and Claim Stipulated Loss Value In this first scenario (abbreviated SESL), you receive the proceeds from selling the equipment, but you must pay off the loan and any accrued interest if it is a leveraged lease.

$$SESL = crf \times SLVC + E \times (1 - s) - (L + AI) \qquad (3.7)$$

where crf = claim recovery distribution function
SLVC = stipulated loss value claim

As mentioned, crf is not a single number but a distribution. The Myerson distribution is used. Data is available from Moody's and Standard & Poor's to specify the 25th, 50th, and 75th percentiles.

Stipulated loss value is the amount the lessee agrees to pay the lessor in the event the lease ends early due to the fault of the lessee. The amount is intended to fully compensate the lessor and is specified in the lease contract for each rent date. The amount that can be claimed is the stipulated loss value (SLV) less the proceeds from the sale of the equipment:

$$\text{SLVC} = SLV - E \times (1 - s) \qquad (3.8)$$

The symbols for equations (3.7) and (3.8) are

> AI = accrued interest
> E = proceeds from sale of equipment. The value of
>   the equipment is not a single number but a
>   distribution of values as specified in equation (2.2)
>   in Chapter 2.
> L = amount of the nonrecourse debt outstanding when
>   the lessee defaults
> s = sales expenses, estimated as a percentage of
>   equipment value; the percentage is lower the more
>   valuable the equipment.

Sell the Equipment and Make Separate Claims This second approach (SESC) allows you to claim tax indemnity on the early sale, commuted rent, and maintenance. The reason for thinking about this scenario rather than simply claiming stipulated loss value is that the sum of the separate claims may be greater than the stipulated loss value.

$$\text{SESC} = crf \times [\text{TISC} + \text{CRC} + \text{MC}) - E \times (1 - s)] \\ + E \times (1 - s) - (L + AI) \qquad (3.9)$$

> where crf = claim recovery distribution function
> TISC = tax indemnity on sale of equipment. The lessor
>   must pay taxes today because the equipment is
>   sold earlier than anticipated. The calculation
>   includes the tax on the sale proceeds today less

the present value of the tax on the sale that was to take place at the end of the lease.

CRC = commuted rent claim

MC = maintenance claim

The tax indemnity claim is specified in equation (3.10).

$$\text{TISC} = \frac{\left[\text{PV}_n(d_{t+1}) - B\right] \times T}{(1 - T)} \tag{3.10}$$

The basis for the commuted rent claim is a comparison of the rent that was contracted for and what the lessor would receive in rent if it went out today and rented the same equipment.

$$\text{CRC} = \text{PV}_m \, (r_t - er_t) \tag{3.11}$$

The maintenance claim assumes that a defaulting lessee returns the equipment in poor condition. Defaulting lessees are known to let maintenance slide.

$$\text{MC} = E_f - [E \times (1 - s)] \tag{3.12}$$

The symbols for equations (3.9)–(3.12) are

AI = accrued interest

B = tax basis of the equipment

(d_{t+1}) = periodic depreciation from the next period until lease end

E = proceeds from sale of equipment

E_f = fair market value of the equipment, if properly maintained, at the time of default

er_t = current fair market rent payments

L = amount of the nonrecourse debt outstanding when the lessee defaults

PV_m = present value at the current pretax market rate

PV_n = present value at the net after-tax yield of the lease

r_t = contractual rent payments

s = sales expenses

T = current tax rate

Enter into a New Lease with Another Lessee   Incorporated in the "new lease" (NL) equation is the assumption that the new rent may be less than the rent on the existing lease. There may also be a difference in the equipment value booked at the beginning of the original lease and the future value estimated after the default takes place.

$$\text{NL} = \text{PV}_i \{ [(ptc_{t+1}) - (1 - rrp) \times r_{t+1}] + E_F \times (1 - s) - R \} \quad (3.13)$$

where PV_i = present value at the implicit rate

ptc_{t+1} = pretax cash from the next period until lease end

rrp = rent reduction percent

r_{t+1} = periodic rent payments as scheduled in the original lease, from the next period until lease end

E_F = proceeds from sale of equipment at the end of the lease

s = sales expenses

R = booked residual

The Nonrecourse Lender Forecloses   When the nonrecourse lender forecloses, takes the equipment, and sells it, you claim on the bases of the broken contract (BCC)and tax indemnity for debt forgiveness (TIDC).

$$\text{FC} = crf \times (\text{TIDC} + \text{BCC}) \quad (3.14)$$

The TIDC claim is applicable to leveraged leases where nonrecourse debt is part of the structure. A foreclosure against equipment subject to nonrecourse debt is treated for tax purposes as a sale of the equipment by the lessor, even though the lessor receives no cash. The lessor records ordinary income earlier than anticipated to the extent that the nonrecourse debt is larger than the tax basis of the equipment. The amount of the claim is calculated on the amount of the loan, unamortized basis, accrued interest, and accrued rent. It backs out the present value of the taxes that would have been paid later had the transaction continued.

$$\text{TIDC} = \frac{[(L - B - AR + AI) \times T] - \text{PV}_n[(p_{t+1} - d_{t+1}) \times T]}{(1 - T)} \qquad (3.15)$$

The breach of contract claim is based on the fact that the lessor will not receive the cash it would have received if the lease went full term. The amount of the claim is based on the after-tax proceeds the lessor would have received on the full lease.

$$\text{BCC} = \frac{\text{PV}_n(atc_{t+1})}{1 - T} \qquad (3.16)$$

The symbols for equations (3.14)–(3.16) are

AI = accrued interest

AR = accrued rent

atc_{t+1} = after-tax cash from the next period until lease end

B = tax basis of the equipment

crf = claim recovery distribution function

(d_{t+1}) = periodic depreciation from the next period until lease end

L = amount of the non-recourse debt outstanding when the lessee defaults

PV_n = present value at the net after-tax yield of the lease

(p_{t+1}) = periodic principal payments from the next period until lease end

TIDC = tax indemnity on debt forgiveness

The Bankruptcy Judge Reaffirms the Lease   The lease contract continues uninterrupted. However, it is appropriate to take some account of the fact that the lease may be reaffirmed (RA) at a reduced rent rate. There is a fair amount of uncertainty about whether a lease will be reaffirmed. The uncertainty is expressed as a weighted probability function whose values are 0 or 1. When 0, there is no reaffirmation and equation (3.17) is not used. When the probability function returns a value of 1, equation (3.17) becomes one of the possible recovery scenarios.

$$RA = PV_i \, [(1 - brp) \times r_{t+1} + E_F \times (1 - s)] \qquad (3.17)$$

where PV_i = present value at the implicit rate

brp = bankruptcy reduced percent

r_{t+1} = periodic rent payments from the next period until lease end

E_F = proceeds from sale of equipment at the end of the lease

s = sales expenses

MODEL RESULTS

Figure 3.10 shows the results of using the recovery model on your leveraged lease of rail cars to CSX. It shows the value of approaching recovery from more than one angle. The scenarios differ considerably.

Chapter 4 integrates recovery, probability of default, and its migration in a model that assesses the risk of a lease over its life.

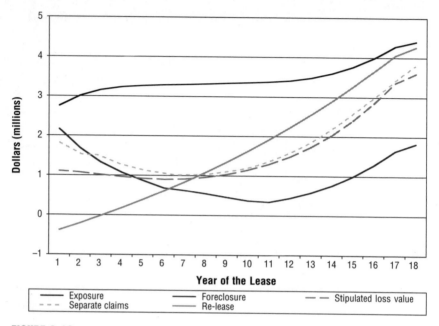

FIGURE 3.10   Exposure and Recovery

A Tool for Risk Pricing Leases

Pricing is a well-established practice in leasing companies. There are a number of software programs that take into account the lessee's cost and cash flow objectives, accounting and tax considerations, and the lessor's financial objectives. These programs produce the lease cash flows shown in Chapter 1. They do not, however, say anything about the risk of a lease. The objective of a tool for risk pricing leases is to allow originators, credit underwriters, and portfolio managers to better understand the risk profile of an individual lease and to adjust the lease structure if the risks are not acceptable.[1] Some risks are judged acceptable because of their return; other risks are too large to be compensated for. A risk pricing tool calculates risk adjusted return on capital, which in turn makes it possible to consistently compare one lease to another, and to compare the risk adjusted returns on leases to returns from any other type of finance, such as loans, bonds, and mortgages.

The risk pricing tool will pull material from the previous chapters on equipment risk, probability of default, migration, and loss-given-default. Figure 4.1, on page 74, shows the risk pricing path. Reading from the left of the figure, today the lessee either defaults or does not default with some probabilities that add up to 100 percent. If the lessee does not default, on the next rent date the same two possibilities exist, but with different probabilities. If the lessee defaults, there is the opportunity of a cure, or the lessee goes into bankruptcy. If the lessee goes into bankruptcy, either the court reaffirms the lease or there is a workout situation. A workout generally results in a loss—the amount you were supposed to get less recovery. The term used is loss-given-default, and it is expressed as a percentage of the amount at risk. The loss is calculated from the probability of default,

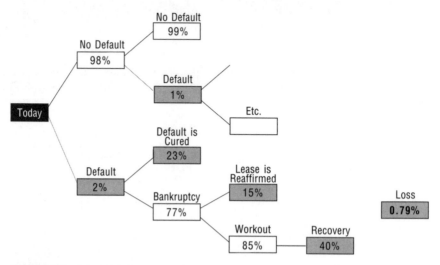

FIGURE 4.1   The Risk Pricing Path

the probability of bankruptcy, the probability of a workout, and the loss-given-default.

The boxes and the lines shaded gray in the figure are the numbers that will be estimated with the risk pricing tool, and they are distributions of values rather than single numbers. The distribution of loss allows you to calculate reserves and capital. The numbers in the boxes are illustrative.

DEFAULT OR NO DEFAULT

A lessee either defaults or does not default. The simplest expression of the two possibilities is a discrete function that establishes the probability that the lessee is in a given state, either default or no default. It is written as follows:

$$DND = D[1, 0: PD_{Rt}, (1 - PD_{Rt})] \tag{4.1}$$

where $DND = 1$ if there is a default and 0 is there is no default
       D = represents a discrete function

PD_{Rt} = probability of default from equation (3.4) in
Chapter 3

The equation acts like a coin flip, but in this case the coin
is weighted by the probability of default. As noted in Chapter 3
the probability numbers can come from Moody's, S&P, from
models, or from your records. The next sections follow the default path.

CURE OR BANKRUPTCY

In the second step, the probability of default is weighted by the
probability that the lessee is able to cure the default, to make up the
missed payment. The information on how often this happens comes
from the lessor's experience dealing with its lessee customer base. It
will be different for each lessor. The terms in equation (4.1) are then
modified by the probability that the default is cured. If there is a
cure it is assumed that you suffer no loss. If there is not a cure the
lessee goes into bankruptcy. PD_{Rt} in equation (4.1) is modified in the
following way:

$$PDc = (1 - PC) \times PD_{Rt} \qquad (4.2)$$

where $\qquad$ PDc = probability of default modified by
$\qquad\qquad\qquad\qquad$ cure
$\qquad\qquad PC$ = probability the default is cured
$\qquad\qquad PD_{Rt}$ = probability of default from
$\qquad\qquad\qquad\qquad$ Equation 3.4 in Chapter 3

For example, if the probability of default is 2 percent and the
probability of curing the default is 23 percent, then the modified
probability of default is

$$1.54\% = (1 - 23\%) \times 2\%$$

REAFFIRMATION OR WORKOUT

In the third step, equation (4.2) is modified by the probability that the lease is reaffirmed by the bankruptcy court. The probability is dependent on the lessor's customer base and on the industry of the lessee. As noted in equation (3.17) in Chapter 3, the reaffirmation can result in the continuation of full rent payments or reduced rent. These considerations modify equation (4.2) as follows:

$$PDcr = (1 - PR) \times PD_{Rt} \qquad (4.3)$$

where $PDcr$ = probability of default modified by cure and reaffirmation
PR = probability of reaffirmation
$(1 - PR)$ = probability the lease goes to workout
PD_{Rt} = probability of default from equation (3.4) in Chapter 3

An example: Starting with the modified probability of default from equation (4.2) of 1.54%, if the probability that the lease is not reaffirmed is 85 percent, then the probability of default is further changed to

$$1.31\% = 85\% \times 1.54\%$$

However, if the lease is reaffirmed at less than the original rent, that difference becomes loss.

ESTIMATED LOSS

The fourth step is to apply the probability of default, modified by the probabilities of cure and reaffirmation, to loss-given-default. To continue with the example, the probability of default modified for cure and reaffirmation is 1.31%; if the loss-given-default in year 10 is $2,000,000, your expected loss is $26,200. This is 0.87 percent of your exposure of $3,000,000. Combining the modified probability of default equation with recovery equations will result in a distribution of losses. From this distribution you can determine the amount of reserves and capital to hold against a lease. The loss distribution is written as follows:

$$LD = EX - PDcr \times \max(SESL, SESC, NL, FC, RAF) \quad (4.4)$$

where   LD = loss distribution
         EX = exposure, stipulated loss value
     PDcr = probability of default modified for cure and reaffirmation
      max = maximum of the variables listed. It is anticipated that you would calculate loss on the basis of the most favorable outcome of the various scenarios.
     SESL = proceeds from selling equipment and claiming SLV, equation (3.7), Chapter 3
    SESC = proceeds from selling equipment and making separate claims, equation (3.9), Chapter 3
        NL = proceeds from a new lease, equation (3.13), Chapter 3
        FC = proceeds from claims following lender foreclosure, equation (3.14), Chapter 3
      RAF = proceeds from a reaffirmation of the lease by the bankruptcy court. This expression combines equation (3.17) in Chapter 3 with the reaffirmation modification.

INPUTS TO THE RISK PRICING TOOL

Tables 4.1 through 4.4 show the inputs that are used in the risk pricing tool. This tool provides a basic outline. It is expected that you would tailor it to your particular circumstances and customer base. For example, you might add information on guarantees that

TABLE 4.1   Risk Pricing Tool—Inputs

Risk Pricing Tool—Inputs

Customer Information		Probability of Cure	
Name	CSX	Average	25%
Credit rating	Baa	Standard deviation	5%
Industry	Rail		
Lease Information		**Probability of Reaffirmation**	
		Average	15%
Type	Leveraged	Standard deviation	5%
After-tax yield	5.26%		
Implicit yield	3.93%	**Claims Recovery Factor**	
Start date	9/30/2006		
End date	12/30/2026	Lower bound	0
		25th percentile	30%
Equipment		50th percentile	56%
		75th percentile	65%
Type	RailCar	Upper bound	100%
Description	Gondola		
Original equipment cost	$20,460,000	**Rent Reduction Percent**	
Residual	20%		
		New Lease	20%
Tax Rate		Reaffirmation	30%
Federal	35%		
State	10%		

affect the credit of the lessee, or residual value insurance that raises the downside value of equipment. The example from your portfolio is your lease to CSX. Table 4.1 lists the basic information on the lease and sets parameters for modifying the probability of default. It also sets the parameters for calculating the amount you will receive when you submit claims to the bankruptcy judge.

Table 4.2 lays out the cash flows that are used in the calculation of loss-given-default. This is a leveraged lease so rent is allocated to (1) interest and principal to the lender and (2) a return on investment to the lessor. In the case of a single investor lease, rent equals the amount received by the lessor. The cash flow sheet can be auto-

TABLE 4.2 Risk Pricing Tool Cash Flow Inputs

	Risk Pricing Tool—Cash Flows					
Year	Rents	Interest	Principal	Lessor	After-Tax Cash	Stipulated Loss Value
0	878,661	878,661	—	—	1,143,146	6,332,891
1	997,916	878,661	119,255	—	1,890,923	6,809,717
2	1,362,028	871,446	490,582	—	1,293,783	7,141,720
3	1,362,028	841,766	520,262	—	861,581	7,372,030
4	1,362,028	810,290	551,738	—	544,968	7,535,104
5	1,362,028	776,910	585,118	—	531,688	7,654,062
6	1,362,028	741,510	620,518	—	517,604	7,730,708
7	1,362,028	703,969	658,059	—	122,556	7,768,330
8	1,362,028	664,157	697,872	—	(273,396)	7,797,349
9	4,465,260	524,011	3,941,249	—	(290,194)	7,849,334
10	1,664,696	343,524	1,321,172	—	(410,142)	7,931,913
11	1,302,875	272,387	1,030,488	—	(553,183)	8,056,986
12	241,214	241,214	—	—	(579,787)	8,238,425
13	241,214	241,214	—	—	(582,930)	8,482,574
14	1,544,089	241,214	—	1,302,875	(582,930)	8,793,292
15	4,361,396	241,214	—	4,120,182	719,945	9,174,195
16	2,297,389	201,174	1,874,402	221,813	3,537,252	7,543,881
17	863,497	82,935	1,483,565	98,196	(395,306)	3,956,639
18	942,665	19,029	629,047	294,589	(564,011)	3,821,420
19	93,145	—	—	93,145	(385,924)	3,736,535
20	—	—	—	—	1,852,221	3,716,950

mated if there are well-established structures for certain types of equipment or customers. The structure would be specified in Table 4.1 and then dropped in automatically.

Table 4.3, on pages 80–81, lists the decay curves and assumed distributions around them for 10 types of equipment; you may need more for your portfolio. The example assumes that you are using a decay curve and volatility parameters obtained from outside sources or you have estimated using your records.

Table 4.4, on page 82, shows the credit inputs. Moody's information is used in this example. Your own records, S&P, or Fitch are

TABLE 4.3 Risk Pricing Tool Equipment Inputs

	Risk Pricing Tool—Equipment									
Inflation										
Equipment Type	1	2	3	4	5	6	7	8	9	10
Annual percent	1.80%	1.90%	0.80%	0.80%	1.70%	–15.00%	1.20%	1.20%	10.00%	1.70%
Equipment Sales Expense (percent of value)										
Equipment Type	1	2	3	4	5	6	7	8	9	10
0 to $5 million	7%	7%	10%	10%	15%	15%	8%	8%	5%	10%
$5 to $10 million	5	5	10	10	15	15	7	7	5	10
$10 to $20 million	3	3	10		15		6	6	5	10
$20 to $50 million	2				15		5	5	4	
More than $50 million	2				15		4	4	4	
Depreciation										
Equipment Type	1	2	3	4	5	6	7	8	9	10
Depreciation life (years)	7	7	5	5	5	5	7	7	Custom	5

Value Distributions

Equipment Type	1	2	3	4	5	6	7	8	9	10
	25th and 75th Percentiles and Bounds (percent of 50th percentile)									
Lower bound	1%	65%	50%	50%	20%	1%	15%	15%	45%	20%
25th percentile	50	77	85	75	65	50	74	74	50	85
75th percentile	100	117	105	105	105	100	128	128	150	115
Upper bound	110	145	110	110	110	100	135	135	200	125
Year	50th Percentile (percent of original equipment cost)									
0	100%	100%	100%	100%	100%	100%	100%	100%	100%	100%
1	93	64	80	75	88	60	94	96	98	65
2	86	55	63	60	77	50	88	91	96	60
3	79	47	50	45	67	30	83	87	95	55
4	73	42	40	30	59	20	78	82	93	50
5	68	36	32	20	51	5	73	78	91	45
6	63	35	25		45		69	74	90	40
7	58	33	20		39		65	70	88	35
8	54	34	16		34		61	66	87	
9	50	31	13		30		57	63	85	
10	46	29	10		26		54	59	83	
11	42				23		51	56	82	
12	39				20		48	52	81	
13	36				18		45	49	79	
14	34				15		42	46	78	
15	31				13		40	43	76	
16	29						37	41	75	
17	27						35	39	74	
18	25						33	37	72	
19	23						31	35	71	
20	21						29	33	70	
21	19						27	32	68	
22	18						26	31	67	
23	17						24	30	66	
24	15						23	29	65	
25	14						21	28	64	

TABLE 4.4   Risk Pricing Tool Credit Inputs

Risk Pricing Tool—Credit

25th and 75th Percentiles and Bounds of Forward Default Rates
(percent of 50th percentile)

Rating	Aaa	Aa	A	Baa	Ba	B	Caa-C
Lower bound	0.001%	0.001%	0.001%	0.001%	0.001%	0.001%	0.001%
25th percentile	100	100	100	50	60	75	90
75th percentile	100	100	265	175	175	135	145
Upper bound	280	270	2500	550	600	725	860

50th Percentile of Forward Default Rates

Year/Rating	Aaa	Aa	A	Baa	Ba	B	Caa-C
1	0.00%	0.00%	0.02%	0.19%	1.22%	5.81%	22.43%
2	0.00	0.00	0.06	0.35	2.15	7.56	17.44
3	0.00	0.03	0.14	0.44	2.53	7.56	16.79
4	0.04	0.09	0.14	0.58	2.63	7.23	14.04
5	0.08	0.08	0.14	0.54	2.67	6.90	12.07
6	0.09	0.09	0.17	0.52	2.53	6.65	11.84
7	0.09	0.08	0.18	0.54	2.10	6.70	10.05
8	0.11	0.10	0.19	0.55	2.15	5.68	12.05
9	0.11	0.07	0.21	0.62	2.11	5.25	9.33
10	0.11	0.07	0.23	0.67	2.10	5.08	8.79
11	0.13	0.08	0.24	0.74	2.38	4.58	7.58
12	0.14	0.15	0.23	0.80	2.64	3.80	0.00
13	0.15	0.17	0.25	0.82	2.69	3.75	0.00
14	0.08	0.24	0.24	0.85	2.58	3.81	0.00
15	0.09	0.13	0.32	0.89	2.29	3.14	0.00
16	0.10	0.14	0.39	0.82	2.64	2.55	0.00
17	0.10	0.21	0.40	0.83	2.38	0.75	0.00
18	0.12	0.19	0.44	0.79	2.32	0.00	0.00
19	0.10	0.29	0.50	0.70	1.85	0.00	0.00
20	0.10	0.25	0.48	0.55	1.79	0.00	0.00

other sources of information on long-term credit ratings and their
distributions. The distributions shown in the first section of the ex-
hibit have two noticeable traits. First, for Aaa and Aa rated companies the distributions are narrow. Second, in the 50th percentile
block of numbers, the initial years of the highly rated companies are
zero; the later years of the lowest rated companies are also zero. Aaa

and Aa rated companies don't default early on; B and C rated companies default early—few make it 20 years.

OUTPUTS OF THE RISK PRICING TOOL

To generate the outputs, the information in Tables 4.1 through 4.4 is combined with equation (4.4), on page 77. Monte Carlo simulation is used to produce 10,000 possible outcomes for every year of the lease. This number of outcomes will exhaust all of the possibilities, given the assumptions made about the equipment, default, claims recovery, cure, and reaffirmation distributions. Figures 4.2, 4.3, and 4.4 focus on recovery and loss-given-default, breaking out the equipment component. Given these results, Figures 4.5 and 4.6 look at the distribution of expected losses in each year.

Figure 4.2 shows the amount of exposure and compares the exposure to how much you can expect to recover, picking the best alternative in each year. It shows that the average recovery exceeds

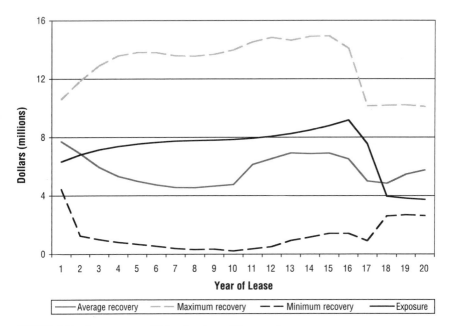

FIGURE 4.2   Exposure and Distribution of Recoveries

exposure for only a couple of years at the beginning and at the end of the lease. The minimum, or worst case, indicates that the amount owed to you is never recovered. On the upside, the maximum, best case indicates your exposure is always covered. The improvement in the later years is the result of declining exposure because your investment is being repaid, and the loan is nearly paid off, giving you a larger claim on the proceeds of an equipment sale.

Figure 4.3 pulls the equipment component out of the recovery and looks at its individual contribution. As is evident, it can be small and is sometimes negative. And only at the end of the lease do the mid values cover the exposure. One reason is that we are looking at equipment net of the claim on it by the lender in the lease. There are circumstances under which the value of the equipment is less than the amount of debt. Recently airline leases have experienced this phenomenon.

Figure 4.4 shows the distribution of loss-given-default, as a percentage of exposure over the life of the lease. In the last chapter we showed how the average recoveries and loss-given-default could behave. The added elements here are the ability to see the

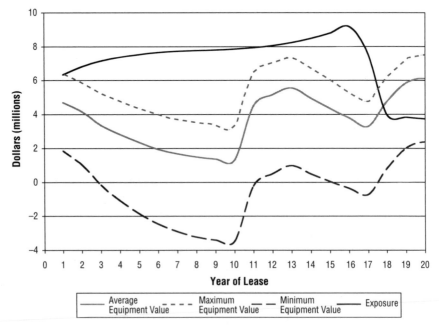

FIGURE 4.3 Exposure and Distribution of Net Equipment Values

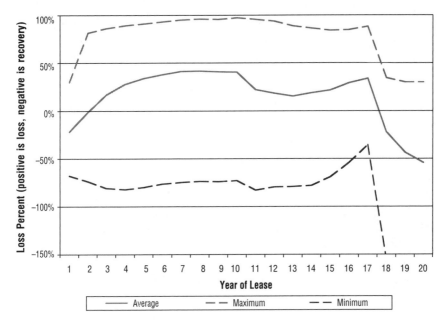

FIGURE 4.4   Distribution of Loss-Given-Default

range of values it can take on, in a given year and over time. All of the possibilities, given the assumptions, are included within the dashed lines. The numbers below zero indicate that the recovery is greater than the exposure, due largely to success in court claims. Figure 4.3 indicates that the equipment, for most of the lease, belongs to the lender. Recall again that this is a leveraged lease; in a single investor lease the equipment belongs to you, but you have more at risk.

As grim as this picture may appear, with an average chance of losing close to half of your investment for most of the lease, these numbers do not take into account the fact that your lessee has more of a chance of surviving and paying rent than defaulting. Figure 4.5, on page 86, takes into account the probability weighted outcomes. The credit quality of your lessees effectively dampens the possibility of the large potential loss-given-default numbers. The range of outcomes is narrowed when the low probability of default is taken into account. The maximum loss is about 3.25 percent.

Given the same lease structure with a single B lessee, the results are very different because of the high probability of default of single

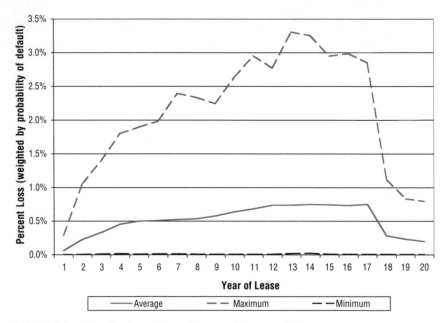

FIGURE 4.5   Distribution of Loss, Baa rated Lessee (CSX)

FIGURE 4.6   Distribution of Loss, B rated Lessee

B companies. The maximum loss-given-default is simulated with the adjusted probability of default. Estimated losses are over 20 percent in some years, as shown in Figure 4.6.

RESERVES AND CAPITAL

From the distribution of losses the reserve and capital percentages can be calculated directly. Reserves are held against what you expect will happen versus what is scheduled to happen. The statistical expression for what you expect is called the *average* or *expected value.* You have lease contracts with 100 lessees under which you are scheduled to receive $1,000 in rent from each, a total of $1,000,000. You know from experience with many lessees that 1 percent of them will not pay. From these contracts you expect to receive $990,000.

From Figures 4.5 and 4.6 it is easy to calculate the amount of reserves you would keep. The amount is the distance between 0 percent loss, the horizontal axis, and the solid gray line. The reserve percent changes every year as all of the elements of the lease change. The principal reason for the difference in the pattern between Baa and B rated lessees is that the probability of default for Baa rated lessees increases as time goes on; for B rated lessees it decreases.

Capital is held against unexpected events—what can happen, but you don't expect to happen. Statistically, the unexpected is the variance around the average. Capital is the distance between reserves and the worst case you want to protect yourself against. One of the standards in the banking industry is to put enough capital aside to protect against 9,997 cases out of 10,000—termed a 99.97 percent confidence interval. This is one of the standards that rating agencies have established for a financial institution to be rated Aa. In the current example we measure capital against the worst case. Most of the distributions in this tool are bounded on the downside so that the worst case and 99.97 percent are nearly indistinguishable.

Figure 4.7, on page 88, shows the reserves and capital numbers

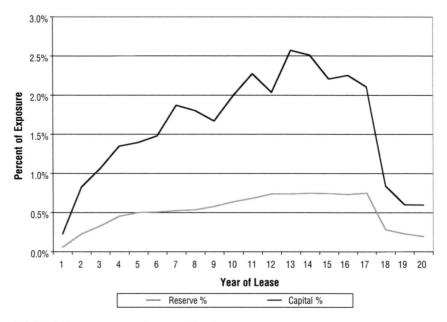

FIGURE 4.7   Reserves and Capital for the CSX Lease

for your Baa rated lessee, CSX. The analysis using a risk pricing tool brings out the changing risks of a lease over time and the changes of reserves and capital needed to keep pace. Whereas many financial institutions plan capital and reserve on a year-to-year basis, it is evident that the risks of leases need longer-range planning.

RETURN

Measuring risk and calculating reserves and capital is the first step in determining whether you are getting paid for the risk you are taking. The basic yardstick is whether you are getting paid at least the rate your capital costs you and enough to cover the reserves that are allocated. The return on the lease in each year is the after-tax cash flow less the cost of funding the investment in the lease. Table 4.5 shows the results for the CSX lease we have been looking at. The return is 7.75 percent, just half of what financial institutions usually expect when they use their capital. Unless your cost of capital is 7.75 percent or less, you should not have entered into this

TABLE 4.5 Return on Risk Capital

Year	1 After-Tax Cash Flow	2 Net Investment	3 After-Tax Interest Rate with Spread	4 Debt Cost of Funding the Investment Balance	5 After-Tax Cash Flow less Cost of Funding	6 Reserves	7 Capital	8 After-Tax Cash Flow Adjusted for Change in Reserves and Capital	9 Lease Risk-Adjusted Return on Capital
0	-4,046,599	5,306,298	1.46%	77,199	-4,123,798	3,703	14,333	-4,140,315	7.75%
1	1,890,923	3,661,073	1.87	67,460	1,823,463	15,427	56,274	1,774,604	
2	1,293,783	2,537,039	2.37	58,295	1,235,488	23,431	75,778	1,211,262	
3	861,581	1,793,833	2.84	48,201	813,379	33,376	99,221	784,069	
4	544,968	1,333,925	2.82	34,687	510,282	37,661	105,072	501,902	
5	531,688	862,807	3.08	23,066	508,622	38,781	113,057	499,977	
6	517,604	380,693	3.34	7,878	509,726	40,466	144,609	477,180	
7	122,556	276,043	3.59	4,890	117,666	41,507	139,959	121,703	
8	-273,396	570,111	3.85	16,936	-290,332	44,907	130,163	-282,542	
9	-290,194	897,175	3.18	23,532	-313,726	49,970	156,764	-343,315	
10	-410,142	1,364,350	3.24	38,335	-448,477	53,968	180,147	-474,219	
11	-553,183	2,002,769	3.30	60,610	-613,793	59,278	163,903	-600,681	
12	-579,787	2,702,745	3.35	83,572	-663,359	60,644	211,758	-712,020	
13	-582,930	3,443,637	3.41	110,297	-693,227	63,179	212,815	-695,779	
14	-582,930	4,224,439	3.47	139,969	-722,900	65,099	194,030	-705,248	
15	719,945	3,718,340	3.53	124,024	595,920	66,945	206,682	582,180	
16	3,537,252	294,075	3.59	4,862	3,532,390	56,403	158,668	3,586,623	
17	-395,306	710,528	3.65	24,726	-420,032	11,184	33,061	-267,746	
18	-564,011	1,322,241	3.71	48,190	-612,202	8,766	22,861	-600,575	
19	-385,924	1,782,612	3.77	66,323	-452,247	7,321	22,323	-450,856	
20	1,852,221	0			1,852,221		22,323	1,856,541	

Notes on the calculations: Columns 1 and 2 are taken from the basic transaction pricing schedules. In column 3 there is an interest rate for each period because the investment balance is funded on a strip basis. This is a way of allocating the true cost to the funding. Column 4 is calculated by multiplying the interest rate in column 3 by the amount of investment not funded by capital (column 2 less column 7). Column 5 is after-tax cash flow less the debt cost of funding (column 1 less column 4). Columns 6 and 7 are taken from the calculations shown in Figure 4.7. Column 8 calculates a net after-tax cash flow by subtracting or adding changes in tax-adjusted reserve levels, and doing the same for capital. Column 9 is calculated as the internal rate of return of column 8.

lease because on its own it is not compensating you for the risk you are taking.

This calculation is done on the basis of the economic cash flows of the lease. The accounting cash flows are different, as shown in Chapter 1, so will produce a different result—often better, because more cash is recognized earlier in the lease.

CHAPTER 5

Tax Risk

There would still be leasing if there were no taxes, but not as much. The lessor owns the equipment and is therefore able to reduce taxable income using the depreciation allowed by the tax code. This represents a significant savings in taxes, most of which is passed on to the lessee. Table 5.1, on page 92, illustrates the tax savings benefits. Depreciation reduces taxable income by $1,000,000. Looking at the totals in the top half of the table, the lessor is taxed on $709,000, not on $1,709,000. Because taxable income is negative, a tax benefit (shown as a positive number in the "Taxes" column) is created. That benefit shelters taxable income from the lessor's other leases or the income of the lessor's parent company. There is also a favorable timing effect. Tax benefits occur during the initial phase of the lease; tax payments are made during the latter phase of the lease. Looked at from today's perspective, that is a good thing. The present value of the tax bill is only 40 percent of total taxes; were taxes distributed according to the rent and residual schedule it would be 65 percent of total taxes.

Tax risk is the uncertainty that the tax rate will remain the same throughout the life of the lease. You don't have the opportunity to go back to the lessee and tell them that you're not making as much money on the transaction because taxes have gone up. The lessee will point out that they are in the same boat; besides, it's not in the lease contract. The bottom half of Table 5.1 shows the effect of a tax increase in the fifth year of the lease. Income on the transaction goes down by nearly 10 percent. The inverse situation also creates tax risk; a tax decrease during the period you are receiving tax benefits reduces your income.

TABLE 5.1 Tax Effect of Owning Equipment

		Original Tax Rate of 35%			
Year	Rent and Residual	Depreciation	Taxable Income	Taxes	Investment and Income
1/1/2005					-1,000,000
2005	166,000	-200,000	-34,000	11,900	177,900
2006	166,000	-320,000	-154,000	53,900	219,900
2007	166,000	-192,000	-26,000	9,100	175,100
2008	166,000	-115,200	50,800	-17,780	148,220
2009	166,000	-115,200	50,800	-17,780	148,220
2010	135,800	-57,600	78,200	-27,370	108,430
2011	135,800	0	135,800	-47,530	88,270
2012	135,800	0	135,800	-47,530	88,270
2013	135,800	0	135,800	-47,530	88,270
2014	135,800	0	135,800	-47,530	88,270
12/31/2014	200,000	0	200,000	-70,000	130,000
Totals	1,709,000	-1,000,000	709,000	-248,150	460,850
		New Tax Rate of 40% Starting 2009			
1/1/2005					-1,000,000
2005	166,000	-200,000	-34,000	11,900	177,900
2006	166,000	-320,000	-154,000	53,900	219,900
2007	166,000	-192,000	-26,000	9,100	175,100
2008	166,000	-115,200	50,800	-17,780	148,220
2009	166,000	-115,200	50,800	-20,320	145,680
2010	135,800	-57,600	78,200	-31,280	104,520
2011	135,800	0	135,800	-54,320	81,480
2012	135,800	0	135,800	-54,320	81,480
2013	135,800	0	135,800	-54,320	81,480
2014	135,800	0	135,800	-54,320	81,480
12/31/2014	200,000	0	200,000	-80,000	120,000
Totals	1,709,000	-1,000,000	709,000	-291,760	417,240

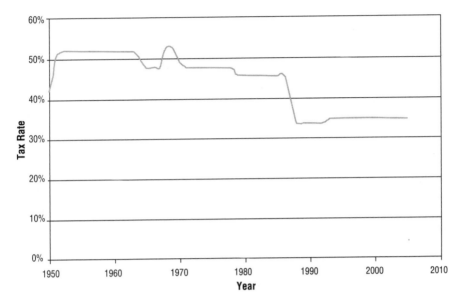

FIGURE 5.1 History of Corporate Tax Rates
Source: IRS, Corporate Income Tax Brackets and Rates, 1909–2002.

In looking back over U.S. history since 1950, tax changes have seemingly occurred randomly. Tax rates have gone up and down over the period, but for long stretches have been fairly stable. Over the last 56 years the federal corporate tax rate, in the highest bracket, has changed only 11 times. It is, however, worth attempting to model the change because of the impact a change has on your income. Having a handle on the risk also makes it possible to plan and do something about it. Figure 5.1 shows the last 56 years of tax history.

MODEL OF TAX RATE CHANGE

As noted tax rate changes are not continuous events like interest rates or stock prices. Since 1950, three of the four increases in rates were related to funding wars—Korea and Vietnam. The tax decreases were promoted as a means to increase economic growth.[1]

One approach to modeling tax rates is a trinomial tree model that branches every year.[2] Three things can happen: The tax rate stays the same, it goes up, or it goes down. The sizes of the movements up and down are different; the probabilities of staying the same or of moving up or down are different. This is depicted in Figure 5.2.

Next year's tax rate is estimated as the weighted probabilities of (1) an increase, (2) staying the same, and (3) a decrease. The specification of next year's tax rate is in equation (5.1) on page 95.

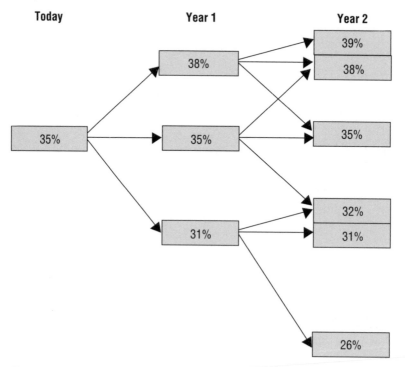

FIGURE 5.2 Diagram of a Trinomial Tree

$$T_{t+1} = (pi_t \times ci_t + ps_t \times T_t + pd_t \times cd_t) \qquad (5.1)$$

where $\qquad$ T_{t+1} = next year's tax rate

pi_t = probability of an increase

ci_t = increased rate

ps_t = probability of staying the same

T_t = today's tax rate

pd_t = probability of a decrease

cd_t = decreased rate

$pi_t + ps_t + pd_t = 1$

For example, using the numbers from Figure 5.2:

$$34.48\% = (.08 \times 37\% + .75 \times 35\% + .17 \times 31\%)$$

The model resamples historical data. It samples both the probabilities of a change and the tax rate levels. The resampling procedure creates 10,000 possible paths that tax rates can take. The historically observed increases range from 1 to 9 percent; decreases, from 1 to 6 percent. For example, in moving from this year to the next, $pd = 13\%$ with $cd = 34\%$ and $pi = 7\%$ with $ci = 36\%$. In moving from next year to the following, $pd = 11\%$ with $cd = 30\%$ and $pi = 8\%$ with $ci = 44\%$. The virtue of this particular modeling process is that it makes full use of the historical information available. It is difficult otherwise to create a distribution with only four tax rate increases and seven decreases.

RESULTS OF THE TAX MODEL

The path traced out by this model and the volatility around it are shown in Figure 5.3. The overall trend is downward, as history

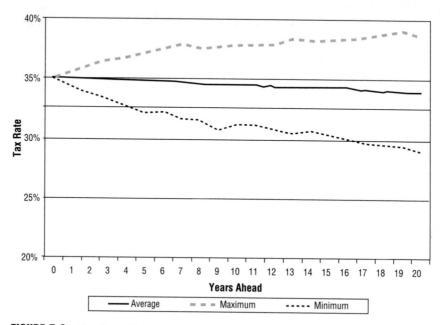

FIGURE 5.3 Tax Rate Change Possibilities

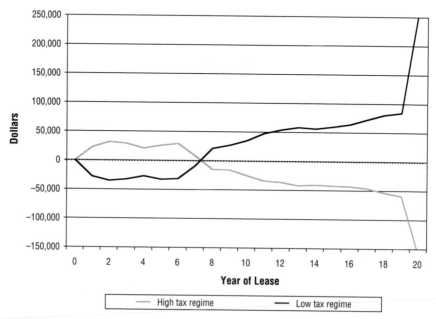

FIGURE 5.4 Tax Risk Effect on CSX Lease—Difference between Scheduled Taxes and High and Low Rates

suggests. The data and the analysis allow for major movements in any year.

The effect of tax rate risk on the CSX lease is shown in Figure 5.4. The preferred order of events would be to have a high tax rate regime during the first half of the lease and a low rate regime in the second half, corresponding to the periods of tax benefits and tax payments. Looking at the figure, below zero there is additional cost; above zero you are saving tax dollars. As you are now in the sixth year of this lease, most of the risk is for rates to rise. If rates were to follow the maximum path over the next 14 years the additional tax expense would be $606,000. The jump at the end of the lease is due to the high scheduled tax bill in the last year; the base from which the change is calculated is much larger.

CHAPTER 6

Options in a Lease

The lessee gets to make all of the choices in a lease—to buy the equipment early or to buy it at the end of the lease, to renew the lease, to renew again, and to buy the equipment at the end of the renewal period. Of course there is a price for each choice, which the lessor sets at the beginning of the lease. This chapter is about these choices, called options, and their worth. Lessors often do not charge for the true value of options because they rationalize, "it's a competitive market and other lessors aren't charging." This chapter is about the cost of this practice to you.

TYPES OF OPTIONS

There are a number of options in lease contracts. The focus of this chapter is those that are quantifiable and represent opportunities for lessors.

Early Buyout Option

The early buyout option (EBO) gives the lessee the right to buy the equipment from the lessor at a specified price on a specified date before the end of the lease. The details are spelled out in the lease contract. If the option is exercised the lessee takes title to the equipment and has no further obligations under the lease. The EBO price satisfies three conditions:

1. If the EBO is exercised, the lessor will receive the same annual yield, but for a shorter period of time.

2. The EBO price must be at least equal to the estimate of the fair market value of the equipment on the EBO date. This, and the following condition, are used to satisfy accounting regulations that the EBO price is not a bargain for the lessee. A bargain purchase price would violate the criteria for obtaining tax benefits for the transaction.
3. The EBO price must be at least equal to the present value of the remaining rents due under the lease plus the estimate of the inflated fair market value of the equipment, on the lease end date.

Purchase Option

A purchase option at the end of the lease comes in two basic forms: fair market value and fixed price. A fair market value purchase option allows the lessee to buy the equipment at the going market price. With some equipment it is easier than others to determine what the fair market price is. Combines fall into the easier category; machine tools and aircraft are more difficult. For the latter, appraisers are called in to value the equipment.

A fixed price purchase option allows the lessee to buy the equipment at a price fixed when the lease was initiated. As with the EBO, the price must reflect the estimated future fair market value of the equipment at the time the lease is drawn up.

Renewal Option

A renewal option at the end of the lease comes in three forms: fair market rent, fixed rent, and renewal plus purchase. A fair market rent renewal allows the lessee to continue to rent the equipment at the going rate for equipment of the same type and age. A fixed rent renewal allows the lessee to continue to rent the equipment at a rate fixed when the lease was initiated. Like the EBO and fixed price purchase option, the renewal rate cannot convey a bargain to the lessee. It is set at a level reflecting what the market would charge for renting equipment of its age and condition. The third form includes the lessee's right to buy the equipment at the end of the renewal period. Valuing this option is the same as for the purchase option at the end of the lease.

VALUE OF A PURCHASE OPTION

The value of the lessee's right to buy the equipment at lease end is the classic valuation of a call option. It is assumed that the lessee will exercise the option to buy the equipment at the end of the lease if the value of the equipment is greater than the purchase option price, plus the premium. If the value of the equipment is less than this, the option is worthless. The equation used here specifies the purchase price, date, and discount rate. The discount rate is used to calculate the value of the option today. The equation is integrated into the equipment valuation model using the decay curve and volatility valuation model discussed in Chapter 2.

$$OV = \frac{\max(0, E - P)}{(1 + d)^t} \qquad (6.1)$$

where   OV = option value at start of lease
      max = maximum function that chooses the highest value within the parenthesis
      E = value of equipment at the end of the lease
      P = purchase price
      d = discount rate
      t = number of years from today to end of the lease

Your lease to Ningbo Fortune Plastic Company includes an option for the lessee to buy the machine for $250,000 at the end of the seven-year lease. The original equipment cost was $750,000. You obtain the decay curve and volatility estimates from an appraiser that specializes in this type of equipment. The inflation estimate is taken from the producer price index series over the last 10 years. Figure 6.1, on page 102, shows where the option purchase price stands in relation to the estimates of the value of the molding machinery. The distribution of values to the right of the dashed line indicates where the option has value. The values of the option are the equipment values, less the purchase price, discounted back to the beginning of the lease. That is shown by the lighter line on the left side of the figure.

You can see that the purchase option begins to have value when the value of the molding machinery begins to exceed $250,000. On

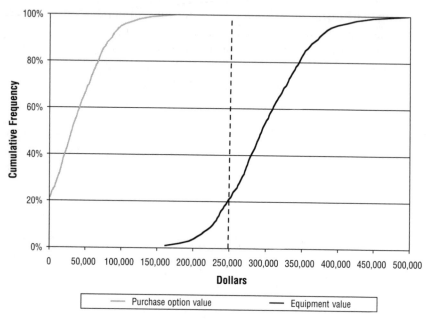

FIGURE 6.1   Value of the Purchase Price Option

average the purchase option is worth $37,700 and with some probability considerably more. This is the amount of money you give the lessee at the beginning of the lease by not charging, explicitly or implicitly, for the purchase option.

A renewal option with a purchase option at the end of it can be evaluated the same as an end-of-lease purchase option. Roll up the renewal rents into the purchase price.

VALUE OF AN EARLY BUYOUT OPTION

In a similar fashion, if there is no charge to the lessee for the EBO, you are giving the lessee money.[1] And in return, if the lessee exercises the option, it is reducing the length of time you will earn a return on your investment.

Calculating the value of the EBO is more difficult than a simple purchase option because there is more than the value of the equipment to consider. If the EBO occurs in the 13th year of a 20-year lease, the lessee is looking at another seven years of fixed-rate financing. The decision to exercise the option will depend on whether the lessee can obtain replacement financing at the same or a better rate. This in turn will depend on the general level of interest rates and the creditworthiness of the lessee 13 years from the start of the lease. It is assumed the lessee is able to use the benefits of depreciation. The option equation says that there is value to the lessee to the extent that the value of the equipment is greater than the early buyout price, and to the extent that the present value of the new financing costs is less than the present value of the lease rent payments. The option equation is specified as follows:

$$OV_{EB} = \frac{\max\{0, [(E - P_{EB}) + R - P_{EB} \times (I + PD \times L)]\}}{(1+d)^t} \qquad (6.2)$$

where OV_{EB} = early buyout option value at the start of the lease

$\max$ = maximum function that chooses the highest value within the brackets

E = value of equipment on the EBO date

P_{EB} = purchase price on the EBO date

R = present value of the remaining rents, from the EBO date to lease end

I = risk-free interest rate for the period: EBO date to lease end

$PD \times L$ = probability of default of the lessee on the EBO date times loss-given-default percent

d = discount rate

t = number of years from today to the date on which the option can be exercised

The probability of default times the loss-given-default percent is used as a proxy for the spread over the risk-free rate that the lessee will pay for financing. The proxy should be reasonably good in a balanced market.

Models to estimate equipment values and probabilities of default are in Chapters 2 and 3. To complete the EBO valuation model, an estimate of future interest rates is needed. That is discussed in the next section.

Interest Rate Model

The interest rate model is a fairly simple one in which the rate in any year reverts toward the average of prior years and features a disturbance term that depends on rate volatility.[2] It is specified as follows:

$$I_t = I_{t-1} + m \times (a - I_{t-1}) + \sigma \times I_{t-1}{}^{\wedge 1/2} \times N\,(0,\,1) \qquad (6.3)$$

where
I_t = interest rate this year

I_{t-1} = interest rate last year

m = mean reversion factor ranging from 0 to 1

a = average rate that is the basis of the reversion—the average of prior years

σ = interest rate volatility, the standard deviation of historical rate series

$N\,(0,\,1)$ = standard normal density function with a mean of 0 and a standard deviation of 1. It is used in conjunction with σ as the engine to generate volatility in the rate estimates.

Figure 6.2 shows the estimate of seven-year risk-free rates from the model over a 10-year horizon.

EBO Valuation Model

Given the formulations for estimating equipment values, interest rates, and default probabilities, a Monte Carlo simulation is run to find the range of values for year 13. These values are then plugged into equation (6.2) to generate a range of option values in year 13. These option values are then discounted to the start of the lease to arrive at the premium that you should charge the lessee for the right to buy the equipment early.

The model is applied to your lease to CSX. The EBO price in year 13 is $12,225,000, the same as the stipulated loss value. The black line in Figure 6.3 shows the value of the EBO on the EBO date. The gray line to its left shows the value at the start of the lease. The output of the model in Figure 6.3 indicates that the EBO has value; the average value of the option is $365,000. This is the

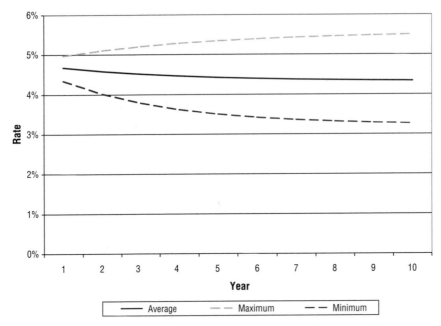

FIGURE 6.2 Estimate of the Seven-Year Interest Rate over the Next 10 Years

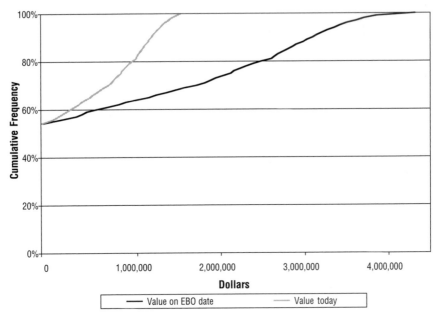

FIGURE 6.3 Values of an Early Buyout Option

estimate of what it is worth to the lessee, and therefore, what you should charge for it.

The value also indicates that it is likely that the lessee will exercise the option to buy the equipment early and deprive you of continued earnings from the lease. It is recommended that lessors evaluate early buyout options periodically. They have an impact on earnings.

CHAPTER 7

Lease Returns

The previous chapters focus principally on the risks in leases. This one looks more closely at return—the components of return and how to separate them. The reason to separate returns is to verify that you are being paid for the risk taken on the entire lease: that the credit risk is covered by the credit return, the equipment risk by equipment return, and the tax risk by the return from the tax cash flows. Knowing what each element contributes to risk and return enables you to do something about it, which will be shown in Chapter 11. There is no need to get rid of the entire lease if one of the risk elements can be reduced, or return increased.

Viewing risks and returns on each component leads naturally to lease valuation. What is a lease worth 5 or 10 years after it has been booked? Knowing how to value a lease allows you to:

- Generate income by selling a lease that has more value to another lessor. For example, the market is telling you that inland barges, new and used, have risen in price. You don't think the rise is permanent, nor will it last until your barge lease ends five years from now, but you want to take advantage of increased barge prices now. A systematic evaluation will tell you if a sale at today's prices is better than holding on to the equipment.
- Accommodate the requests of existing customers. An existing lessee, a railroad, wants to lease more of the same equipment, a singular type of locomotive. Your credit and equipment capacity for the lessee is nil. An evaluation shows that you can accommodate the lessee by selling off one of the leases in portfolio, at a

profit. The evaluation can also tell you if the new lease more profitable to you than leases you already have in portfolio.

SEPARATING THE RETURNS

Returns are separated into those attributable to credit, equipment, and taxes. The procedure is to calculate the present value of the three cash flow streams from the evaluation year to the end of the lease. The cash flow streams used are pre-tax cash flows, less the residual; the residual; and cash taxes. The cash flow streams are modified to isolate the tax effect of the lease arrangement. Tax cash flows are summed by year from the start of the lease until the year in which the sum equals zero. Thereafter, cash taxes are subtracted from pre-tax cash flows and, at the end of the lease, taxes are subtracted proportionately from pre-tax cash flows and the residual. The discount rate for the cash flows is the net after-tax yield of the lease. It is used because it is consistent with the rate at which the transaction was funded and it is the rate at which the transaction earns.

Your locomotive lease to SNCF is an example for the leveraged lease. The lease was originated in 1989 and runs until 2014. The locomotives cost $92 million. The contribution of each element is valued in three different years (1, 10, and 16) until the end of the lease. Table 7.1 shows what this looks like. (The cash flows on which the results are based are in the Appendix to this chapter, Table 7.4, on page 118.) At inception the lease has a return of $27 million on a present-value basis. The contribution of the tax cash flows is the greatest—60 percent of the value of the lease is reflected in the deferral of taxes. On a net basis, taxes in the transaction are not paid until 2011. By year 10, tax benefits have turned to tax payments; the tax component is now a burden and creates a negative value for the lease. In year 16, as the lease is maturing, the value of the lease is again positive with credit cash flows and the equipment value offsetting the tax burden.

In contrast, the characteristics of the single investor lease are fairly uniform throughout its life. This is your lease of bookbinding equipment to RR Donnelley. The lease was originated in 2005 and runs until 2015. The machinery cost $20 million. The contribution of each element is valued in three different years (1, 5, and 8) until

TABLE 7.1 Returns to Credit, Equipment, and Tax

25-year Leveraged Lease			10-year Single Investor Lease		
Year 1 Returns			**Year 1 Returns**		
Credit	$ 9,748,482	35%	Credit	$16,600,666	87%
Equipment	1,362,502	5%	Equipment	2,000,996	11%
Tax	16,458,238	60%	Tax	400,050	2%
Total lease	27,569,221	100%	Total lease	19,001,712	100%
Year 10 Returns			**Year 5 Returns**		
Credit	$11,267,668	738%	Credit	$ 9,994,166	83%
Equipment	3,234,426	212%	Equipment	2,722,333	23%
Tax	−16,029,750	−1049%	Tax	−709,964	−6%
Total lease	−1,527,656	100%	Total lease	12,006,535	100%
Year 16 Returns			**Year 8 Returns**		
Credit	$18,655,274	197%	Credit	$ 4,841,480	59%
Equipment	5,433,420	57%	Equipment	3,429,355	41%
Tax	−14,598,802	−154%	Tax	0	0%
Total lease	9,489,892	100%	Total lease	8,270,836	100%

the end of the lease. Table 7.1 shows what this looks like. (The cash flows on which the results are based are in the Appendix to this chapter, Table 7.5, on page 119.) The return on the total lease never becomes negative on a present-value basis. The cash flow returns to credit are always the dominant feature of the lease; tax cash flows at inception are worth 2 percent of the returns on the lease, are negative in the middle, and toward the end of the lease are not a factor.

This is a broad look at the valuation tool. Refinements will take into account three factors:

1. The risk that the cash flows scheduled at the beginning of the lease do not happen as planned due to changes in credit, equipment values, or tax rates. The unplanned changes can be positive, like an increase in the price of inland barges, or negative, like an increase in the tax rate.
2. Funding costs—debt and capital. Debt is allocated to the entire lease; there is no basis for allocating it to the individual

components. Capital, on the other hand, can be individually allocated as it is derived from the risk numbers.

3. A different discount rate. Changing interest rates and lessee credit rating may make a different rate appropriate.

CALCULATING THE RISKS

The risk pricing tool in Chapter 4 is used to estimate credit and equipment risks. The tax model in Chapter 5 is used to estimate tax risk. In all cases, risk is measured as the difference between scheduled cash flows and the worst possible case. During the lease the separation of risks is not clear-cut between credit risk and equipment risk. To the extent that equipment is used to reduce loss in event of default, it has value beyond what it can be sold for at the end of the lease. Equipment values and risks are not stripped away from credit considerations until the end of the lease.

Risks are compared to the present value of the flows from the three components. The risk calculations are slightly different. For credit risk the highest loss from evaluation year to the end of the lease, on a present-value basis, is used. It would be incorrect to sum up the estimated losses in each year of a lease in calculating credit risk. For equipment, the risk that the residual will not be realized is estimated at the end of the lease. The difference between the estimated value of equipment at lease end and the booked residual is present-valued to the evaluation year. For taxes, the worst-case tax scenario is estimated for each year, and the difference between that number and the scheduled tax payments is calculated. The series of these differences is present-valued to the evaluation year. Tax risk is calculated differently than the others because these changes will occur every year.

Table 7.2 sums up the risk calculations and compares them to the return calculations in Table 7.1. In the leveraged lease, tax risk dominates, reflecting its importance in this structure. In the single investor lease, credit risk dominates. For both leases the credit risk is fully compensated by credit returns. Equipment risk in both leases grows as time goes on. The present value of the equipment return increases as you move closer to the end of the lease, so the same

TABLE 7.2 Returns and Risks to the Components of Leases During their Lives

25-Year Leveraged Lease

Year 1

	Returns	Risks	Risk/Return
Credit	$ 9,748,482	$ 62,900	0.65%
Equipment	1,362,502	75,438	5.54%
Tax	16,458,238	1,321,896	8.03%
Total Lease	27,569,221	1,460,235	5.30%

Year 10

	Returns	Risks	Risk/Return
Credit	$11,267,668	$ 126,275	1.12%
Equipment	3,234,426	164,250	5.08%
Tax	-16,029,750	1,479,283	-9.23%
Total Lease	-1,527,656	1,769,808	-115.85%

Year 16

	Returns	Risks	Risk/Return
Credit	$18,655,274	$ 86,864	0.47%
Equipment	5,433,420	275,919	5.08%
Tax	-14,598,802	1,610,580	-11.03%
Total Lease	9,489,892	1,973,363	20.79%

10-Year Single Investor Lease

Year 1

	Returns	Risks	Risk/Return
Credit	$16,600,666	$228,722	1.38%
Equipment	2,000,996	181,623	9.08%
Tax	400,050	77,500	19.37%
Total Lease	19,001,712	306,222	1.61%

Year 5

	Returns	Risks	Risk/Return
Credit	$ 9,994,166	$289,120	2.89%
Equipment	2,722,333	249,105	9.15%
Tax	-709,964	59,300	-8.35%
Total Lease	12,006,535	597,525	4.98%

Year 8

	Returns	Risks	Risk/Return
Credit	$ 4,841,480	$218,011	4.50%
Equipment	3,429,355	315,661	9.20%
Tax	0	0	0.00%
Total Lease	8,270,836	533,672	6.45%

movement in price is magnified. On a risk/return basis there is hardly any change.

Tax risk and return are easy to think about in the beginning of the lease. Both returns and risks are positive. As the present value of the tax cash flows become negative, the interpretation of return is difficult. It is hard to think of tax as not contributing to the lease, yet from these vantage points it pulls down the yield and adds to the risk. The risk measure indicates how much larger the tax number could get in the worst case. Tax risk is carried by the returns on credit and equipment.

What do you do with this information? In the case of the leveraged lease, you now know how exposed you are to tax risk. In the first years the tax structure provides an earnings boost; thereafter taxes represent a cost and one that has the most possibility for changing an earning lease into a losing one. In the case of the single investor lease, you know the magnitude of your exposure to equipment risk throughout and its potential for dramatically reducing the profitability of the lease. Chapter 11 sets out some solutions.

TO SELL OR HOLD

That is the question.[1] If you wish to sell, you would like to satisfy two criteria:

1. The proceeds from the sale are greater than the proceeds from holding the lease on your books.
2. There will be an accounting gain from the sale, or at least not a loss if the economics are good.

To Hold

Most of the considerations about holding the lease have been looked at in the previous sections of this chapter. Two additional issues are:

1. Incorporating the current market estimate of equipment value.
2. Subtracting the debt and capital costs of funding the lease from the returns.

The value of holding a lease from today until maturity is the present value of its after-tax cash flows less the costs of capital and debt used to fund it. The amount funded is the investment balance of the lease, which can also be expressed as the sum of the after-tax cash flows remaining in the lease. The amount of capital is derived from the risk calculations. The amount of debt is the difference between the investment balance and capital. Also included is an estimate of future equipment values. The calculations result in an after-tax number. The equation looks like this:

$$HV = PV\,(ATC) + PV\,[(E - R) \times (1- T) \\ - C \times Cc - (IB - C) \times Cd \tag{7.1}$$

where HV = value of holding the lease until maturity
          PV = present value at the after-tax yield, from the evaluation year until lease end
     ATC = after-tax cash flows
        E = distribution of estimated equipment values
        R = booked residual
        T = tax rate
        C = capital for credit, equipment, and tax risks, calculated as in the previous section
      Cc = cost of capital (15 percent is used here)
      IB = investment balance
  $IB - C$ = amount of debt
      Cd = after-tax cost of debt

This evaluation does not mark-to-market the lease. This evaluation estimates what the lease is worth to you if you keep it in portfolio until it matures. A mark-to-market calculation would include changes in the discount rate, the rent, the debt rate, the lessee's creditworthiness, and the residual to reflect current market conditions.

Table 7.3, on page 114, gives an example of how the numbers look for the single investor lease in year 5 with the expectation that you will be able to sell the book presses for at least the *average* estimated value, $5,047,920. The risk adjusted return to you for holding the lease is $10,524,662.

In Chapter 4 the return on a lease was adjusted for the amount of capital used in calculating the return on risk adjusted capital.

TABLE 7.3 Equation for Hold Value

HV	equals	PV (ATC)	plus	E	R	(1 – T)	minus		C	Cc	minus		IB	C	Cd
		12,006,524		PV	5,047,920	4,000,000	(1 – .35)	PV	597,525	15%	PV		12,229,640	597,525	3.00%
									580,124	15%			10,236,120	580,124	3.50%
									550,345	15%			9,141,400	550,345	3.75%
									533,672	15%			7,955,840	533,672	4.00%
									510,111	15%			6,671,860	510,111	4.50%
									505,254	15%			5,281,320	505,254	4.75%
10,524,662	equals	12,006,525	plus	484,079			minus		417,965		minus		1,547,977		

This is another way of incorporating risk into the return; calculate the cost of risk capital in each year and deduct it from the return.

Or to Sell

The four considerations in estimating the sale price of the lease are:

1. The buyer's ability to depreciate the equipment. That is a benefit for the buyer that you should take into account.
2. The buyer's tax rate—it may be different from yours.
3. The value of the equipment. It is different from today's perspective than it was five years ago.
4. Interest rates and the creditworthiness of the lessee. These may have changed since the lease started. The changes are reinforced by the shortened tenor of the lease. At inception the lease to RR Donnelley was for 10 years, and now you are selling a 5-year lease.

To estimate the price you will receive, first calculate the pre-tax price of the lease using an updated residual and discount rate and take account of the buyer's ability to depreciate the equipment. The solver function in MS Excel makes the calculation easy to do. Link the new price to the depreciation schedule. Add rent and the new residual to calculate taxable income, then taxes. Rent and taxes create a new cash flow series. The price the buyer pays is the present value of the cash flow series at the new discount rate.

Then calculate the after-tax price by adjusting the pre-tax price for accruals (rent and interest if it is a leveraged lease) and the remaining basis in the equipment. Then apply taxes. The equation that spells this out is

$$\text{ATP} = PTP - (PTP + A - B) \times T \qquad (7.2)$$

where ATP = after-tax price
        PTP = pre-tax price
          A = accruals. Accrued interest is added; accrued rent is subtracted. This element is necessary if the evaluation date is different than the rent or interest dates. For simplicity it is assumed there are no accruals in the following calculations.

B = basis. Basis is the original equipment cost less depreciation taken. State and federal depreciation rules differ for some equipment so it may be necessary to separate the tax calculation into two, one for state and the other for federal tax.

T = tax rate. If the federal and state basis are the same the combined tax rate is used. If not, they are calculated individually.

Your lease to RR Donnelley is used as the example. The equipment is assumed to have the same value as in the hold analysis. State and federal bases are assumed to be the same. The federal tax rate of 35 percent is used. But interest rates have fallen since the lease began, the maturity is shorter, and the creditworthiness of RR Donnelley has improved so that the market yield for this lease is 6 percent, not 8.2 percent.

The price the buyer should be willing to pay is $17,440,000, assuming he is thinking the same way about the equipment, interest rates, and the lessee. Of that, $1,684,000 is due to the fall in interest rates.[2] The amount you will receive after paying taxes is

$$\$11{,}739{,}200 = 17{,}440{,}000 - (17{,}440{,}000 - 1{,}152{,}000) \times .35$$

This is about $1.2 million more return than if you hold the lease on your books. But more than that amount, nearly $1.7 million, is the result of falling interest rates, not any particular change in the lease. If you decide to sell, you need to think about the debt underlying this lease, if you have funded it at a fixed rate. If you repay the underlying debt there would be a cost of about $430,000 for every 1 percent difference between current rates and the original funding rates. If you repay the debt you have a direct expense now; if you hold it and use it for another lease you are foregoing profit over time.

Accounting

The economics of a sale seem to work, assuming the difference in funding costs is not terribly large. However, you would like to do a transaction that not only makes good economic sense but also makes good accounting sense. To get to the accounting bottom line for the sale, some further adjustments need to be made. You will show an accounting gain if your sale price, with adjustments for the investment balance, deferred taxes, and cash taxes, is a positive number. Equation (7.3) shows more formally how this looks:

$$AV = PTP - IB + DT - (PTP - A - B) \times T \qquad (7.3)$$

where AV = accounting value
         PTP = pre-tax price
           IB = investment balance
        DT = deferred taxes
          A = accruals
          B = basis
          T = tax rate

For your RR Donnelley lease, this looks like:

$$\$3,358,560 = 17,440,000 - 12,229,640 + 4,049,000$$
$$- (17,440,000 - 1,152,000) \times .35$$

On an accounting basis the sale shows a profit. And it is larger than the $2.9 million that would have been booked over the next five years if you held the lease.

The value of making an evaluation is to:

- Know if you will make money on the sale, versus holding the lease in portfolio.
- Know why you are making money—interest rates, residual, other.
- Ensure that the economically good thing to do is also good for accounting.

APPENDIX—LEASE CASH FLOWS

Tables 7.4 and 7.5 illustrate the cash flows used in calculating risk and return on the SNCF and RR Donnelley leases, respectively.

TABLE 7.4 Annual Cash Flows for SNCF Lease

Lessee Name: Societe Nationale Chemins de Fer
Original Equipment Cost: $92,012,688
Equipment Description: GE Dash 9 Locomotives

Year Beginning	Purchase, Loan & Residual		Fees	Rent	Interest on Loan	Principal Repayment	Pretax Cash Flow	Cash Tax	After-Tax Cash Flow
Jan 1989	-92,012,688	Purchase	-1,295,226	0	0	0	-33,126,722	5,184,264	-27,903,692
Jan 1989	60,181,192	Loan draw					-33,126,722	5,184,264	-27,903,692
Jan 1990	-10,465,419	Loan repayment	0	3,790,923	-6,304,450	12,978,946	0	9,794,125	9,794,125
Jan 1991	0		0	3,952,206	-6,622,936	2,832,013	161,283	7,235,263	7,396,546
Jan 1992	0		0	7,743,129	-6,871,726	3,080,803	3,952,206	4,178,569	8,130,775
Jan 1993	0		0	7,743,129	-7,038,239	1,225,340	1,930,230	3,018,639	4,948,869
Jan 1994	0		0	11,125,965	-6,979,230	-4,146,736	-1	1,754,562	1,754,561
Jan 1995	0		0	7,692,790	-6,715,334	-977,456	0	2,904,463	2,904,463
Jan 1996	0		0	7,687,605	-6,609,471	-1,078,134	0	1,212,985	1,212,985
Jan 1997	0		0	7,685,805	-6,496,623	-1,113,087	76,095	-482,404	-406,309
Jan 1998	0		0	7,698,566	-6,394,736	-865,300	438,530	-527,524	-88,994
Jan 1999	0		0	7,697,256	-6,304,299	-890,746	502,211	-628,781	-126,570
Jan 2000	0		0	9,307,870	-6,102,472	-3,028,236	177,162	-1,300,412	-1,123,250
Jan 2001	0		0	9,282,683	-5,765,376	-3,517,306	1	-1,427,712	-1,427,711
Jan 2002	0		0	9,264,025	-5,384,436	-3,879,589	0	-1,574,766	-1,574,766
Jan 2003	0		0	9,243,446	-4,964,259	-4,279,187	0	-1,736,967	-1,736,967
Jan 2004	0		0	9,220,747	-4,500,804	-4,719,943	0	-1,915,875	-1,915,875
Jan 2005	0		0	9,195,710	-3,989,613	-5,206,097	0	-2,113,210	-2,113,210
Jan 2006	0		0	9,168,095	-3,425,769	-5,742,325	1	-2,330,871	-2,330,870
Jan 2007	0		0	9,137,634	-2,803,850	-6,333,784	0	-2,570,950	-2,570,950
Jan 2008	0		0	9,104,037	-2,117,872	-6,986,164	1	-2,835,758	-2,835,757
Jan 2009	0		0	18,048,606	-879,042	-17,068,784	100,780	-6,609,603	-6,508,823
Jan 2010	0		0	9,463,824	0	0	9,463,824	-3,804,457	5,659,367
Jan 2011	0		0	9,463,824	0	0	9,463,824	-3,804,457	5,659,367
Jan 2012	0		0	9,463,824	0	0	9,463,824	-3,804,457	5,659,367
Jan 2013	0		0	9,463,824	0	0	9,463,824	-3,804,457	5,659,367
Jan 2014	0	Residual	0	0	0	0	19,782,728	-7,952,657	11,830,071
Totals	-42,296,915		-1,295,226	211,645,523	-106,270,537	-49,715,772	-1,276,921	-8,758,185	-9,957,574

TABLE 7.5 Annual Cash Flows for RR Donnelley Lease

Lessee Name: **RR Donnelley**
Original Equipment Cost: **$20,000,000**
Equipment Description: **Timmons T48 Book Presses**

Year Beginning	Purchase & Residual	Rent	Pretax Cash Flow	Cash Taxes	After-Tax Cash Flow
Jan 2000	−20,000,000	0	−20,000,000	237,920	−19,762,080
Jan 2001	0	3,320,200	3,320,200	1,077,920	4,398,140
Jan 2002	0	3,320,200	3,320,200	181,920	3,502,140
Jan 2003	0	3,320,200	3,320,200	−355,680	2,964,540
Jan 2004	0	3,320,200	3,320,200	−355,680	2,964,540
Jan 2005	0	3,320,200	3,320,200	−547,580	2,772,620
Jan 2006	0	2,716,540	2,716,540	−950,780	1,765,740
Jan 2007	0	2,716,540	2,716,540	−950,780	1,765,740
Jan 2008	0	2,716,540	2,716,540	−950,780	1,765,740
Jan 2009	0	2,716,540	2,716,540	−950,780	1,765,740
Jan 2010	4,000,000	2,716,540	2,716,540	−1,400,000	5,316,540
Totals	−16,000,000	30,183,660	14,183,660	−4,964,280	9,219,380

CHAPTER 8

Diversification

When you book your first lease, you make judgments about the ability of the lessee to make the rent payments, the future value of the equipment, and the stability of tax rates. When you book your second lease, you make the same judgments about another lessee, the future value of another type of equipment, and taxes. In addition, you think about the interaction between the two leases. Are the lessees likely to have payment problems at the same time, or are their industries so different that this is unlikely? Will the prices of the equipment in each lease rise and fall together, or will the price of one move up while the other moves down? For each subsequent lease, you continue to judge individual lease risks, but the number of relationships among them grows dramatically. A portfolio of 10 leases with two risks each has 100 separate relationships. This is good, because if each relationship is affected by a different economic or financial event, your portfolio will not collapse from a single event.[1]

TYPES OF DIVERSIFICATION

Lease portfolios have a number of sources of diversification—different lessees, different equipment types, equipment coming off lease at different times in the economic cycle, and tax benefit and tax payment periods occurring at different times. This diversification reduces the overall risk of a leasing portfolio. If you have $1 million of risk in a lease to an airline and $1 million of risk in a lease to a railroad, your total risk is not $2 million—it is less. How much less depends on how the financial fortunes of the two companies relate to one another and the extent to which prices of aircraft and prices of railcars move together.

Your sample portfolio contains a lease of a 737-800 to Ryanair and the lease of rail cars to CSX. The companies serve different markets—one serves passengers in Europe; the other, freight in the United States. The companies are generally rated differently in terms of operational efficiency. The 737-800 is not a substitute for the railcars. If there were no relationship between the companies or the equipment, your risk would be about $1.4 million (calculated using equation 8.1, on page 124). Diversification reduces risk, thereby reducing the amount of capital needed to cushion you against risk, and increasing the returns of the leasing business.

The factors that influence the financial health of the railroad (grain harvests, coal mining) are different than those that affect the financial health of the airline (oil prices, tourist travel). So you would not expect the companies to default on their rent payments at the same time, nor would you expect the price cycle of railcars to be similar to that of airplanes.

The analysis extends to companies in the same industry. Even though two airlines have many things in common, there are differences such as reservation systems, routes, equipment used, and markets served. Because of those differences, even the sum of the risks of two airline leases, one to Ryanair and one to Singapore Airlines, is less than the parts.

The extent of diversification between two lessees depends on how they react to changes in the macro variables (coal shipments, interest rates, retail sales), what variables affect them most significantly, and the extent to which the companies may be able to ride through up and down cycles.

Leases of the same equipment start and end at different times. You have railcars coming off lease every other year for the next 10 years. Over those 10 years railcar prices may rise, fall, rise, and fall again. Not all of your railcars will face falling markets. And, as noted in Chapter 7, you have the tools to evaluate whether you should sell now, before the next downturn.

There is a relationship between lessee industries and the equipment used by those industries, particularly transportation—airlines, railroads, and trucking. When airlines are doing well, the prices of used aircraft are high; when airlines do poorly, the prices of used aircraft are low—so low that you can't even give them away and they are parked in the desert. And there are the times in between, when airline credit and aircraft prices move somewhat independently of one another. The effects of diversification change depending on the health of the industry.

Another source of diversification is taxes. Leases go through two periods: At the beginning of their lives tax benefits are created, and thereafter tax payments are made. An increase in tax rates is beneficial to you during the benefit phase, detrimental during the payment phase. The mix of leases in the portfolio and their time profile determine the net effect of a tax change on your portfolio. A good mix reduces the impact of any change in rates.

CORRELATION

The measure most often used to measure diversification in a portfolio of leases is the correlation coefficient. The correlation coefficient is a number between −1 and +1 that measures the degree to which two things move together. At +1 they are perfectly in sync. At −1 they move in completely opposite directions. At 0, the movement of one has no relation to the movement of the other.

Depiction of Correlation and Diversification

Starting with a portfolio of two leases, we can visualize correlation and the effects of diversification with the use of lines and triangles.[2] Think of the length of each line in Figure 8.1 as representing the

Risk A

Risk B

FIGURE 8.1   Depiction of Risks

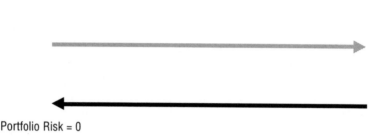

Portfolio Risk = Risk A + Risk B

FIGURE 8.2   Correlation Coefficient of 1: No Diversification

Portfolio Risk = 0

FIGURE 8.3   Correlation Coefficient of −1: Total Diversification

amount of risk in lease A and the amount in lease B. In this example the risks are equal.

With a correlation coefficient of 1, the two risks are affected by exactly the same factors and they move together. Even though they are two leases they act as one. Figure 8.2 shows this in terms of the risk lines.

With a correlation coefficient of −1, the two risks move in opposite directions in response to a change in the same factors, like interest rates and coal prices. There is no risk in a portfolio with these two leases. Figure 8.3 shows this in terms of the risk lines.

A correlation coefficient of 0 means that the two risks are affected by entirely different economic and financial events so they have no relation to one another. There is no pattern to their movement. The risk of the portfolio is then less than the sum of the two risks, as shown in Figure 8.4. The portfolio risk can be expressed as

$$\text{Portfolio Risk} = (\text{Risk A}^2 + \text{Risk B}^2)^{1/2} \qquad (8.1)$$

The more usual case is where there is some correlation between the risk of two lessees, like utilities with gas-fired power plants and airlines, as in Figure 8.5. They are both affected by energy prices, but also by a number of different factors. From geometry you'll recognize that portfolio risk is the same as the formula

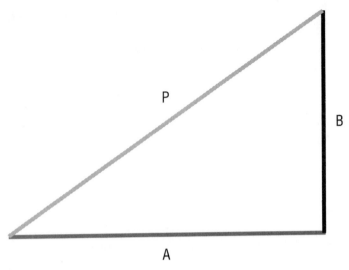

FIGURE 8.4 Correlation Coefficient of 0: No Relationship

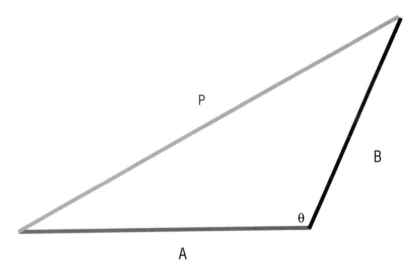

FIGURE 8.5 Correlation Coefficient of 0.4: Some Relationship

for the side of a triangle. The correlation coefficient is the cosine of the angle opposite the side.

$$\text{Portfolio Risk} = (\text{Risk A}^2 + \text{Risk B}^2 - 2 \times \text{Risk A} \times \text{Risk B} \times \text{cosine } \theta)^{1/2} \qquad (8.2)$$

Portfolio risk does not increase by the same amount even when adding another lease, as shown in Figure 8.6, on page 126. The dark dashed line is shorter than the light dashed line.

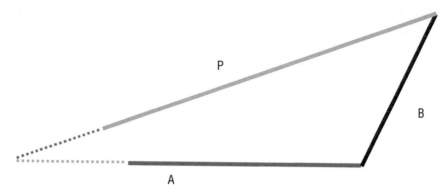

FIGURE 8.6   Correlation Coefficient of 0.4: Adding a New Lease with Risk A

Equations for Correlation and Portfolio Diversification

Correlation measures the degree to which, for example, interest rates that affect the risk of lease A move with crude oil prices that affect the risk of lease B. The correlation coefficient is calculated by comparing a time series of interest rates with a time series of oil prices. The equation for the correlation coefficient is

$$\rho_{AB} = \frac{\sigma_{AB}}{\sigma_A \times \sigma_B} \qquad (8.3)$$

where ρ_{AB} = correlation coefficient between interest rates and crude oil prices

σ_{AB} = covariance between interest rates and oil prices. The term "covariance" is defined in the Appendix.

σ_A = standard deviation of interest rates. The term "standard deviation" is defined in the Appendix.

σ_B = standard deviation of oil prices

The risk of a portfolio of two leases, combining equation (8.2) and equation (8.3) is

$$\text{Portfolio Risk} = (\sigma_A^2 + \sigma_B^2 + 2 \times \sigma_{AB} \times \rho_{AB})^{1/2} \qquad (8.4)$$

where σ_A^2 = the standard deviation of interest rates squared (standard deviation squared is also known as *variance*)

σ_B^2 = the standard deviation of oil prices squared

σ_{AB} = covariance between rates and oil prices

ρ_{AB} = correlation coefficient between interest rates and crude oil prices

Equation (8.4) will be generalized to more than two leases in Chapter 10.

Estimating Correlation Coefficients for Credit

You want to know whether two lessees are going to default together. If Calpine defaults, what is the likelihood that JB Hunt will also default? What is the correlation coefficient? What is the joint probability of default? The problem with finding the answer is that there is very little historical evidence about companies defaulting together. However, there are a couple of approaches you can use to estimate the likelihood of lessees defaulting together: factor correlation and asset correlation.

Factor correlation identifies the key cost and revenue factors for a lessee or a lessee's industry, then maps these factors to market prices and indices.[3] Each lessee has a weighted set of costs and revenues. Correlation coefficients between the market prices and indices are calculated. Then you can compare your lessees, Calpine and JB Hunt, and find the correlation coefficient. Table 8.1, on page 128, is an example of the three steps: calculate the correlation coefficients between the factors, assign weightings to the factors for each lessee, and map the correlation coefficients to the factor weightings. The mapping first considers the common factors, then allocates the remainder proportionally.

The correlation matrix spells out the relationships between each

TABLE 8.1 Calculation of Correlation Coefficient between Calpine and JB Hunt

Correlation Matrix				
	Coal Prices	Gasoline Prices	Lumber Prices	Insurance Premiums
Coal Prices	1	0.4	0.2	0.2
Gasoline Prices	0.4	1	0.1	0.8
Lumber Prices	0.2	0.5	1	0.6
Insurance Premiums	0.2	0.8	0.6	1

Weightings of Factors		
Factors	JB Hunt	Calpine
Coal Prices		60%
Gasoline Prices	20%	20%
Lumber Prices	30%	
Insurance Premiums	50%	20%

Mapping JB Hunt to Calpine		
Factor	Weight	Correlation
Gasoline Prices	20%	1
Insurance Premiums	20%	1
Lumber Prices to Coal Prices	30%	0.2
Insurance Premiums to Coal Prices	30%	0.2
Correlation JB Hunt and Calpine		0.52

pair of factors. Reading down the first column of the Correlation Matrix block, coal prices are clearly related on a one-to-one basis with coal prices. For every one-dollar movement in coal prices, gasoline prices move 40 cents, lumber prices move 20 cents, and insurance premiums move 20 cents. Because the correlation coefficient between coal prices and gasoline prices is the same as between gasoline prices and coal prices, and so forth, the top and bottom sides of the diagonal, marked by 1s, are mirror images of one another. Reading down the second column, for every one-dollar change in gasoline prices, coal prices move 40 cents, lumber prices 50 cents, and insurance premiums 80 cents. (The numbers have been created as an example).

The correlation coefficient of 0.52 is used in an equation with the individual probabilities of default for JB Hunt and Calpine to arrive at a joint probability of default. The equation that gives you the joint probability of default is

$$PD_{AB} = BN\ (Z_A, Z_B, \rho_{AB}) \qquad\qquad (8.5)$$

where PD_{AB} = joint probability of default of lessee A and lessee B

BN = bivariate normal distribution. The term "bivariate normal distribution" is defined in the Appendix.

$Z_A = N^{-1}\ (PD_A)$, inverse normal distribution of the probability of default of lessee A. The term "inverse normal distribution" is defined in the Appendix.

$Z_B = N^{-1}\ (PD_B)$, inverse normal distribution of the probability of default of lessee B

ρ_{AB} = correlation coefficient between the factors affecting lessee A and lessee B

Here's how this works in practice. JB Hunt has a one-year default probability of 0.19 percent; Calpine has a one-year default probability of 5.81 percent; and their correlation coefficient is 0.52. However, the probability that they default together is only 0.1 percent. If they were totally unrelated to one another, the probability of defaulting together would be 0.01 percent, 10 times less. If they were perfectly correlated to one another, the probability of defaulting together would be 5.81 percent since if Calpine defaulted, so would JB Hunt.

An asset correlation approach to joint default probability has been developed by CreditMetrics.[4] It uses asset correlation coefficients and default probabilities to estimate a joint default probability. The default probabilities are from Standard & Poor's and Moody's. Asset correlations are based on country and industry; for example, German steel versus French utilities, or German steel versus U.S. chemicals. They are calculated by using time series of historical equity return indices.

The next step is to assign a country and industry weighting for each lessee, and a measure of nonsystematic (idiosyncratic) risk. The idiosyncratic risk is related to the total assets of the lessee. It is reckoned that the smaller the lessee, the more it will depend on its individual characteristics and the less it will be affected by overall events in its industry and market. For large lessees, the opposite is the case. As an example of how weightings are assigned, one lessee might be mapped as 80 percent United States and 20 percent Europe; 70 percent railroads and 30 percent shipping. This will give the lessee a 56 percent weight in U.S. railroads, 24 percent in U.S. shipping, 14 percent in European railroads, and 6 percent in European shipping.[5] Given the country/industry correlations, the lessee weightings, and the individual lessee default probabilities, the joint probability of default is calculated using equation (8.5).

The factor correlation and asset correlation methods have different underlying drivers and calculate their correlations differently. The factor approach assumes that the underlying economics of operating the company is the best way to ascertain the synchronicity of two lessees. The asset correlation approach assumes that equity prices will contain all the information necessary to assess co-movement. The advantage of CreditMetrics' asset correlation approach is that it is supported by an online software program and a data gathering team.[6]

Estimating Correlation Coefficients for Equipment

You may have a reasonable amount of data in the equipment department on the prices different equipment were sold for, and there are a number of times series available from appraisers, auctioneers, and specialists, at a price.[7] One caution in using them: Because all equipment prices are affected by inflation, they all usually have an upward trend. This will give any two series of prices a higher correlation coefficient than is appropriate. The two solutions are (1) to deflate the series with a price index, or (2) to calculate the correlation coefficient using the year-to-year price changes as the series.

A reasonable substitute for used equipment price series are producer price indices, publicly available at no cost.[8] The producer price indices are for new equipment, not the used equipment you are most interested in. The argument for using these series is that there is a fair amount of substitution potential between new and old equipment, so the prices of used equipment will tend to follow the prices of the new; you are concerned with the relationship between two series of prices, so their absolute level is not important. The same caution applies about adjusting them for inflation.

With equipment there is a second source of diversification: the time the equipment comes off lease. Forklifts coming off lease in 2007 will not face the same market as those coming off lease three years later, in 2010. The supply and demand factors will have changed. An analysis of your own data and time series provided by auctioneers and appraisers can confirm this and allow you to develop a measure of diversification from this source. Figure 8.7 is an example of the analysis of sales price data on combines. Seven-year-old combines ranged in price from 25 to 55 percent of original cost, depending on the year they were sold.

If the only sources of data are producer price indices, the correlation coefficients for time diversification can be estimated by running the correlation year T against year (T + 1), year T against (T – 1), and so on. From past experience, I can attest there is not much

FIGURE 8.7 Sales Prices of Equipment—Variation in Prices of Equipment the Same Age Depending on Year of Sale

value in estimating correlation coefficients more than three years forward and three years back.

ONCE DIVERSIFIED, ALWAYS DIVERSIFIED?

Correlation coefficients are the means used to measure the diversification of a portfolio of leases, and they are necessary when thinking about a portfolio. But they are single numbers. They can change, and sometimes they change quickly. The Russian debt crisis in the summer of 1998 showed that U.S. mortgage-backed securities can be highly correlated with Russian government bonds. Prior to the crisis you would have assumed a very low correlation. Figure 8.8 gives another illustration. The first differences of the producer price indices for gas turbines and transportation equipment were correlated over 16 years, 1987 to 2002. The average was –0.08, as indicated by the dashed line. Looking at individual two-year periods,

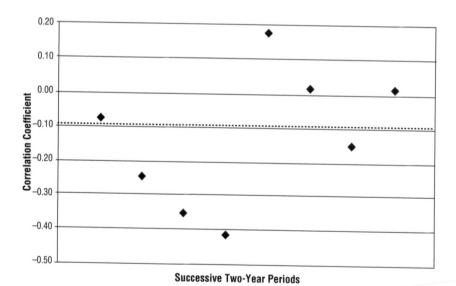

FIGURE 8.8 Correlation Coefficients of Gas Turbine and Transportation Equipment Prices, 1987–2002
Source: U.S. Department of Labor, Bureau of Labor Statistics.

however, you can see that the correlation coefficient has ranged from –0.45 to 0.18. There are three fairly distinct groupings of coefficients—those that are significantly negative, those that cluster around zero, and one that shows positive correlation.

So you need ways to think about how and when correlation changes, and what the changes mean for your portfolio. The finance world has addressed the issue with the use of copulas. A copula is a function that joins two distributions, like the equity indices of German steel and U.S. chemicals or of turbine and transportation equipment prices. A copula can be defined to extend across the entire range of correlation possibilities. However, they are not particularly easy to use in a portfolio setting.[9]

One way of thinking about correlation coefficients that change is to use different coefficients for different periods. Think about the volatility of what you are using to establish the correlations—stock indices or revenue and cost factor prices. In periods of normal volatility, you have one set of correlation coefficients; in periods of high volatility you have a second set of coefficients; and in periods of extreme volatility you have a third set of coefficients.[10] Going from average to extreme volatility, the correlation coefficients generally rise. There is a reasonable amount of literature on the relationship of volatility and correlation.[11] Using more than one set of correlation coefficients gives you a better picture of how diversified your portfolio is under different circumstances. In Chapter 10 the effect of changing correlation coefficients on portfolio choice is shown.

PROBABILITY OF DEFAULT AND EQUIPMENT VALUES

Another correlation to think about is the one between probability of default and equipment values. Earlier in this chapter the transportation sector was singled out as one where the financial condition of the lessees and the value of equipment were intertwined. The reason for thinking about this relationship is that it affects loss-given-default, the amount of capital allocated to a lease, and the return on the lease. One way of expressing the relationship of equipment and credit is by mapping the distribution of default probabilities into the distribution of equipment values. The three scenarios are:

1. Probability of default low, equipment prices high.
2. Probability of default high, equipment prices low.
3. Probability of default average or normal, equipment prices average/normal.

The process for linking probability of default and equipment values consists of three steps:

1. Establish the distributions for the probability of default and equipment values and decide where the scenarios fit within the distribution
2. Break the equipment value distribution into three separate distributions.
3. Link the probability of default distribution to the equipment values distribution with the following MS Excel statement:

$$\text{IF (PD} < 0.1\%, \text{HEV, IF (PD} > 5.8\%, \text{LEV, MEV))} \qquad (8.6)$$

where   PD = probability of default
        HEV = high equipment value, scenario 1
        LEV = low equipment value, scenario 2
        MED = mid equipment value, scenario 3
        0.1% = upper boundary for low default probability, scenario 1
        5.8% = lower boundary for the high default probability, scenario 2

Figure 8.9 compares the Monte Carlo simulation of the default probabilities with the corresponding equipment values. The equipment values for low default probabilities (less than 0.1 percent) are high ($700,000 to $850,000); the equipment values for high default probabilities (greater than 5.8 percent) are low ($125,000 to $325,000); and there is the great mass in the middle.

This provides an understandable picture of the different scenarios in the trucking, airline, and railroad leasing sectors.

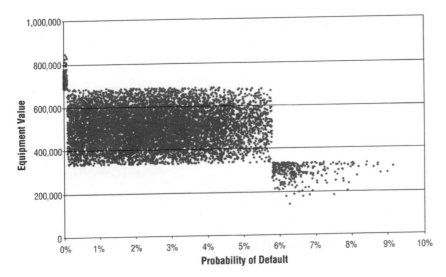

FIGURE 8.9 Probability of Default and Equipment Values

APPENDIX—STATISTICS DEFINITIONS

This section contains the definitions of some of the statistical terms used in this chapter.

Covariance

Covariance is a measure of the co-movement of two time series around their averages. The higher the number, the more the two series move together. The equation for covariance is

$$\text{Cov}_{AB} = \Sigma(A_i - A) \times (B_i - B) \tag{8.7}$$

where A_i = a number in series A
  A = average of series A
  B_i = a number in series B
  B = average of series B

One way of conceptualizing this is to think of a rectangle with a series of points: A_1B_1 is one point, A_2B_2 is another, and AB is another.

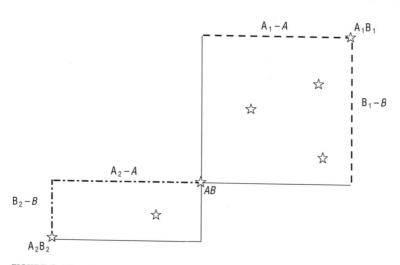

FIGURE 8.10 Illustration of Covariance

The expression $(A_1 - A) \times (B_1 - B)$ is the area of the rectangle. The covariance measure sums up the rectangles; some have positive signs, others have negative signs. To the extent that the signs are mostly positive, as shown in Figure 8.10, the co-movement is high.[12]

Standard Deviation

The standard deviation is a measure of the spread around the average value in a series. It is calculated in four steps:

1. Calculate the difference between the average and each of the numbers in the series.
2. Square each of those numbers.
3. Add up all of the squared numbers—that is called the *variance* of the series.
4. Take the square root of the variance.

In a normal distribution, one standard deviation around the average contains about two-thirds of the cases in the distribution.

Three standard deviations around the average contains 99.7 percent of the cases in a normal distribution. If the distribution is not normal, the standard deviation is not as predictive of the number of cases, particularly beyond one standard deviation.

Bivariate Normal Distribution

A bivariate normal distribution describes the situation where, for each number in series A, the corresponding numbers in series B are normally distributed. The elements of the equation for the distribution include the standard deviations of each series, their covariance, and the correlation between them. Figure 8.11 is a picture of a bivariate normal distribution.

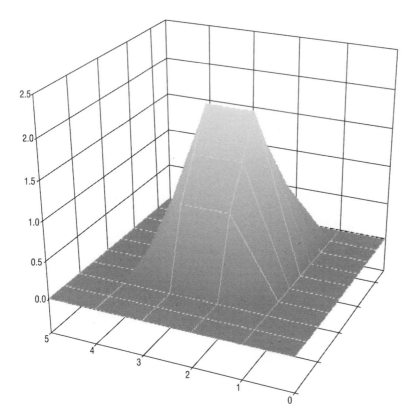

FIGURE 8.11 Illustration of a Bivariate Normal Distribution

Inverse Normal Distribution

The inverse normal distribution function converts a normal probability (percentage) into a value for a given mean and standard deviation. For example, for a normal distribution where the mean is 0 and the standard deviation is 1, 25 percent of the time the values in the distribution will be below −0.67. If the mean is 3 and the standard deviation is 1, 25 percent of the time the values will be below 2.33.

CHAPTER 9

Factor Analysis

This chapter expands on the use of factors in estimating correlations and presents a different way of looking at the credit risk of a lessee. It does this by looking at current market prices and indices that will affect the income statement and cash flow—the underlying elements of the lessee's ability to pay rent. Factor analysis[1] tells portfolio managers what is happening to their lessees long before financial statements are received and analyzed. It is an early warning system. The signals from factor analysis are often six to nine months ahead of the analysis of financial statements. Financial statement analysis only confirms what did happen. Too often it is too late to take appropriate preventative measures if there is a problem.

The standard way of looking at concentrations in a portfolio is to focus on the exposures to specific industries. Most financial institutions that extend credit perform some sort of industry analysis. Factor analysis provides another take on concentration. It tells portfolio managers a different story than traditional industry analysis about where their true concentrations lie.

Factor analysis first identifies the key factors affecting the costs and revenues of a lessee. It then maps them to observable market prices and indices. And finally, it tracks price movement. The mapping of the underlying factors to market prices is the key feature of this analysis and the ingredient that allows it to be an early warning system.

An example is a wheat farmer who leases tractors and combines. On the cost side, key factors are the gasoline for the trucks and tractors, seed, and interest on loans. Gasoline futures and interest rate futures, as well as freight rates, are reasonable predictors of what it is costing the farmer to grow the wheat and move it to market. On the revenue side, the key factors are the price of wheat coupled with the amount he produces. A good indicator of the price of wheat is wheat futures prices. Futures prices estimate now what the farmer is likely to receive for the crop when it is harvested in the coming months. Price movements affect the farmer's profits: A rise in gasoline futures prices will reduce profits; an increase in wheat futures prices will increase profits.

Current prices dictate what the farmer is paying for inputs and receiving for his product today. Futures prices reflect the consensus of market participants about what the lessee will face in the future. Though certainly not infallible, market prices and price indices are the best predictors available, and assuredly, breakouts from a trend indicate changes in market fundamentals. In addition, there is evidence that sharp increases in the volatility of prices are good predictors of market stress.[2] These changes call for a closer look by portfolio managers at what they imply for the financial condition of lessees. Some may have sufficient margins to withstand adverse changes in key costs or revenues; others will not.

ORGANIZING THE ANALYSIS

Initially, it is easier to start with industry breakdowns. The four steps involved are:

1. Identify the principal industry groups in the portfolio.
2. List the important lessees in each group.
3. Determine the most important revenue and cost factors.
4. Map the factors to market prices and indices.

Identify industry groups in the portfolio by the North American Industry Classification System (NAICS) code. It is generally not necessary to drill down to the six-digit level; three to four digits are usually enough. For example, in most portfolios it is sufficient to specify 313—textile mills. Specifying 313111, yarn spinning mills or 313113, thread mills, is probably not necessary.[3]

Identify the lessees that represent most of the exposure in each industry group. Listing the lessees may suggest splitting up a given industry sector, going to a more detailed code. For example, some of the power plants in the portfolio may be coal fired and some are natural gas fired. For one, the price of coal is significant; for the other, the price of natural gas. Or in the technology group, some of the lessees may be computer manufacturers; others may be software developers. They are separated because the principal factors affecting their costs and revenues are different.

Identify the three or four most significant cost and revenue factors from Bureau of Economic Analysis's input-output tables.[4] Determining the cost factors from the input-output tables, "Commodity-by-Industry Direct Requirements" is fairly straightforward. The size of the coefficient is the criteria for choosing the factors.

Determining the revenue factors requires more information. The table is titled "Industry by Industry Total Requirements." It is set up to tell you how important one product is to the manufacture of another product or service. Another way of saying this is, who is an industry selling its output to. For example, the table shows that coal is sold to both the aluminum industry and the cement industry in the United States. In fact, coal is more important to the aluminum industry than to the cement industry; the input coefficient is larger. But the cement industry in the United States is twice the size of the aluminum industry, so cement outranks aluminum as a revenue source for coal. In addition to knowing the input coefficients, it is necessary to know the size of the industry the product is being used in.

Another place to find information on the revenue and cost factors is the prior annual reports of the lessees, particularly the income statement and report to shareholders. The income statement indicates the large cost categories; the report to shareholders will tell you the types of customers the lessee is selling to.

Map the cost elements and revenue factors to current prices, futures prices, stock indices, or other economic indicators that are readily available and are published at least monthly. Examples include heating oil futures prices, consumer confidence index, electricity prices, labor costs in the construction industry, premium index in the insurance industry, producer price index for computer peripherals, and stock index for the auto industry. The principal sources for prices and indices are INO.com (about 75,000 futures, options and stock prices); the online service from Yahoo; the Bureau of Labor Statistics; and economagic.com (about 200,000 economic time series). Other indices, such as rail freight traffic trends and truck tonnage, are found on industry-specific sites. The Appendix to this chapter contains a table that lists most of the factors, prices, and sources that leasing companies use. Included are the web sites of the sources just mentioned.

The next step is to review the movement of the prices and indices representing the factors on a monthly basis. It is unlikely that the number of different factors will exceed 75 to 100 regardless of the size of the portfolio.

EXAMPLE OF THE ANALYSIS ON YOUR PORTFOLIO

Table 9.1 shows how the analysis might be organized highlighting some of the industries in your portfolio, as well as other industries. The first two columns list the factor and what type or class of factor it is.

The "Factor Importance" column denotes the factor's weight in the portfolio. It is the sum of the industry exposures for each factor divided by the total exposure in the portfolio. (Then multiply by 100 to get whole numbers.) A factor numbered 1 or A does not count for more in the calculation than a factor numbered 2 or B. Factor importance is the field that shows the exposures of the portfolio to underlying economic forces. In this sample portfolio the largest factor components are coal, grain, and petroleum (diesel fuel and natural gas prices). The evolution of prices in these fundamental commodities will have the most significant impacts on this portfolio. This analysis shows that the true concentrations in this portfolio lie not in the railroad and utility industries as the exposure numbers would suggest, but elsewhere.

"Factor Change" indicates the change (annualized) in price or price index in three different periods: the one-year period, six months back; the last six months; and the last month. One year, six months back is chosen as a baseline period. Price changes in this period have been largely absorbed by the lessee, and their effects on the lessee's income are known and have been analyzed. The more recent changes are currently being absorbed into the lessee's cost and revenue structure and have not been reported. This aspect provides portfolio managers with early warnings of impending problems.

TABLE 9.1 Factor Analysis Tracker

Legend — Revenues: 1, A Costs: A

		Industry Exposure	Railroads	Plastics	Electric Utilities—Coal	Electric Utilities—Gas	Truck Transportation
	Revenues		$438,500,000	$63,100,000	$78,602,000	$150,000,000	$231,450,000
	NAICS		482	4831	221112	221112	4841
	Labor Coefficient		0.37	0.13	0.13	0.13	0.218

		Factor Importance		Factor Change							
Factor Name	Factor Class	Revenue	Cost	One Year, 6 Months Back	Last 6 Months	Last Month	Railroads	Plastics	Electric Utilities—Coal	Electric Utilities—Gas	Truck Transportation
Coal prices	Futures		8	2.2%	4.0%	1.2%			A		
Coal production	Output index	46		3.2%	1.5%	0.5%			2		
Cooling people	Futures	24		2.0%	5.0%	1.5%				2	
Electricity prices	Price index		7	10.0%	10.0%	5.0%					
Food and drink	Output index	7		2.0%	5.0%	1.0%					
Freight rates—rail	Price index		15	2.9%	6.2%	1.9%	1	B	B		
Freight traffic trends	Index	46		4.0%	4.7%	1.4%		1			
Grain production	Output index	46		7.5%	-4.0%	1.2%		C			
Heating people	Futures	24		5.5%	-0.1%	0.0%	3		1	1	
Home sales—new	Index	7		15.0%	15.0%	-4.0%	2		3	3	
Industrial output	Output index	24		-3.0%	2.0%	0.4%		2			
Insurance premiums	Price index		31	9.5%	8.5%	1.7%					B
Motor vehicle parts	Price index		24	-4.5%	-2.5%	-0.5%					C
Petroleum—Diesel	Futures		76	3.0%	15.1%	3.0%	A	A			A
Petroleum—Natural gas	Futures		13	2.6%	14.3%	2.9%				A	
Pipeline transportation	Price index		13	3.1%	3.5%	0.7%				B	
Railroad rolling stock	Price index		46	-4.8%	-4.5%	-1.8%	B				
Retail sales	Index	24		-1.0%	-2.0%	-0.8%					3
Truck tonnage	Index	24		3.4%	4.2%	1.3%					1
Wholesale trade	Index	24		-3.7%	-2.3%	-0.7%					2

EXTENSIONS OF BASIC FACTOR ANALYSIS

Factor analysis at the broad industry level is a first step in increasing your ability to more actively monitor your lessees' financial health. Subsequent steps may include:

- Analysis of individual lessees above a specified exposure amount. It is certainly worth knowing if the lessee that accounts for one-quarter to one-third of the exposure in the industry has different factors, perhaps due to geography or customer base, than the industry as a whole.
- Greater attention to where the lessee operates. Electricity prices move quite differently in different regions of the United States; a dramatic example is California in 2000.
- Analysis of each new lessee, coupled with a software program that identifies lessees when one or more factors change significantly. Each lessee file contains factor flags that are raised when an important change occurs.
- An econometric analysis of factor change and income variability of industries and large companies. This allows the lessor to attach specific weights to the factors affecting each industry. A reasonable estimate of the portfolio impact of a $5 increase in the price of diesel fuel can then be made. The usual approaches to determining the factors are principal component analysis and its close cousin, factor analysis. The analyses are statistical techniques for determining which factor explains the greatest variance in a lessee's financial performance, then finding the next most important, the next, and so on until the variance is sufficiently explained.

BENEFITS

The principal benefit of factor analysis is that it gives you, the lessor, an idea today of what may happen in the future, and enables you to take action today.

This organized approach enables you to easily track which industries are affected when any relevant factor moves suddenly. Positive as well as negative trends can be tracked.

This analysis also shows how the fundamental economic movers affect the overall portfolio. Factor analysis can point out where the real concentrations and correlations in the portfolio lie. Often the concentrations extend outside of the general understanding of how one industry is related to another. This has implications for which industries may get in trouble together.

Another benefit of mapping the factors to market prices and indices is that the data to perform the analysis is readily available, and generally of fairly high quality. Also, the time series are fairly long so that it is possible to back-test assumptions.

Factor analysis is not unique to equipment financing portfolios; it can be used for any type of portfolio. It is a bridge for evaluating portfolios of different instruments—loans, leases, securities—together.

APPENDIX—FACTORS, PRICES, AND SOURCES

Table 9.2 is a compilation of many of the cost and revenue factors that influence lessees' income. Most of the factors are mapped to prices that can be readily tracked. In addition, a number of the factors are mapped to production or output indices. They are particularly useful at times for tracking revenues. Most of the sources can be accessed without cost on the Web.

TABLE 9.2 Factors, Prices, and Sources

Factor	Futures/Prices	Source	Production/Output	Source	Other Indices	Source
Airline industry	Price index	www.bls.gov/ppi/home.htm www.ino.com				
Aluminum	Futures	www.futures.tradingcharts.com www.ino.com				
Cattle	Futures	www.futures.tradingcharts.com	Production	www.usda.gov/nass		
Chemical	Price index	www.bls.gov/ppi/home.htm	Output index	www.economagic.com		
Coal	Price index	www.bls.gov/ppi/home.htm	Production	www.eia.doe.gov		
Commodities (2,000 covered)						
Consumer confidence	Price index	www.bls.gov/ppi/home.htm			CCI	www.pollingreport.com/consumer.htm
Cooling people	Futures	www.climetrix.com www.ino.com				
Corn	Futures	www.futures.tradingcharts.com www.ino.com	Production	www.usda.gov/nass		
Cotton	Futures	www.futures.tradingcharts.com www.ino.com	Production	www.usda.gov/nass		
Crude, light sweet	Futures	www.futures.tradingcharts.com www.ino.com				
Diesel	Futures	www.futurestradingcharts.com				
Electricity	Prices	www.economagic.com www.ino.com	Output	www.economagic.com		
Gasoline	Futures	www.futures.tradingcharts.com www.ino.com				
Heating oil (jet fuel proxy)	Futures	www.futures.tradingcharts.com				
Heating people	Futures	www.climetrix.com www.ino.com				
Hogs, lean	Futures	www.futures.tradingcharts.com	Production	www.usda.gov/nass		
Industry outputs (600 covered)	Price index	www.bls.gov/ppi/home.htm				
Insurance industry						
International trade	Premiums	http://data.bls.gov/ppi/home			Imports of goods	www.economagic.com

Factor	Futures/Prices	Source	Production/ Output	Source	Other Indices	Source
Leading indicators					Leading indicators	www.economagic.com
Lumber	Futures	www.ino.com www.futurestradingcharts.com				
Natural gas prices	Futures	www.ino.com www.futures.tradingcharts.com				
New and existing home sales					House sales	www.economagic.com
Pipeline transportation	Price index	www.bls.gov/ppi/home.htm				
Petroleum production			Output index	www.economagic.com		
Railcar orders					Orders and deliveries	www.rsiweb.org
Rail freight traffic trends					Traffic trends	www.railwayage.com
Railroad industry	Railroad price index	www.bls.gov/ppi/home.htm				
Refinery output			Production	www.economagic.com		
Rental and leasing costs (interest rates)	Futures	www.ino.com www.futures.tradingcharts.com				
Retail sales					Sales	www.economagic.com
S&P 500	Price index	www.ino.com www.futures.tradingcharts.com				
Ship and boat new orders					New orders	www.econstats.com
Steel	Stainless steel metallics prices	www.cruspi.com				
Stock price indices (all)					Indices for all industries	finance.yahoo.com
Titanium	Prices	www.metalprices.com				
Truck new orders					New orders	www.econstats.com
Truck tonnage					Truck tonnage index	www.truckline.com
Turbine and turbine generator sets	Price index	http://data.bls.gov				
Wheat	Futures	www.ino.com www.futures.tradingcharts.com	Production	www.usda.gov/nass		
Wholesale trade					Trade numbers	www.consus.gov/svsd/wholsmon/view/historic.txt

CHAPTER 10

Portfolio Risk and Return

This chapter is about combining the risks, returns, and correlations of the leases in your portfolio into a single framework to determine the return of the overall portfolio and the risks you are taking to get that return. A portfolio model is designed to:

- Aggregate and quantify credit, equipment, and tax risks of the entire portfolio (and portfolio segments) to direct the origination, syndication, and secondary market activities.
- Determine the return and risk contributions of an individual lease in a portfolio context, which can then be used to drive origination through incentives geared to risk and return.
- Compare return to risk ratios for a variety of portfolio segments—industry, equipment, credit rating, time of origination, lease type—to be used as a tool in evaluating acquisitions.
- Estimate the diversification effects of different lessees and different equipment types under different diversification scenarios to drive capital allocation.
- Construct hedges on an aggregate risk basis as well as on an individual lease basis.
- Consider all of the above over the life of the leases in the portfolio.

The quantifiable benefits of this analysis are:

- *Reduce the cost of capital.* Many leasing companies are allocated capital from their parent companies. The allocation is generally not the result of having measured the risks of the leasing portfolio. A portfolio model provides a definable measure of risk to defend a different, typically lower capital allocation. Portfolio samples indicate that risk is reduced by a factor of four to five when diversification is taken into account explicitly. To the extent that capital can be reduced by even 1 percent, on a $5 billion portfolio with a cost of equity of 15 percent, the annual savings would be $7.5 million.

- *Increase return of new leases.* Most leasing companies optimize pricing with respect to lessor and lessee objectives and accounting and tax constraints. A portfolio model allows a leasing company to ascertain the marginal contribution of the lease to the portfolio after having been priced for risk (Chapter 4). If the risk pricing discipline is able to generate another 10 basis points on a 10-year $20 million transaction, that is worth $200,000. If the diversification effects of a new transaction are such that you can comfortably lower pricing and win the transaction, that can be counted as additional income. Risk adjustment can work in the other direction as well, eliminating unattractive transactions that otherwise may have been done.

- *Measure the benefit of hedges.* Through segment analysis, a portfolio model can determine which segments contribute the most risk to the portfolio. If it is determined a specific segment has too much risk, entering into credit swaps could diversify the portfolio and reduce risk at little to no cost. Consider a portfolio with significant rail risk. Here, swapping the credit exposure of a group of railroads for the credit risk of a group of utilities may reduce the aggregate credit risk of the portfolio. A portfolio model determines the benefit of such a transaction.

  Assume two rail leases of equal size, each with a credit risk of $10 million. The diversified aggregate risk of these two leases is $19.8 million (using a correlation coefficient of 0.95). However, one $10 million rail lease and one $10 million utility lease will have an aggregate credit risk of only $15 million (using a correlation coefficient of 0.15)—a risk reduction of nearly $5 million and a consequent reduction in the cost of capital.

PORTFOLIO THEORY

Classical portfolio theory says that you have an efficient portfolio when the assets in your portfolio are aligned so that for every dollar of return you have the least amount of risk. At that point it will also be true that for every dollar of risk you have the most return.[1] The following is an example of a portfolio of three lease types you may consider putting in your portfolio, with different returns and risks and the correlations between them.[2] The basic information is shown in blocks A and B of Table 10.1, on page 152. In this example the definition of risk is standard deviations of the returns.

In this chapter the standard deviation is used as the measure of risk. In the previous chapters risk is defined as the distance between the average of the distribution and the tail of the distribution (worst case). There is value in looking at leases in a portfolio context in terms of standard deviation as a measure of risk. Nearly all of portfolio theory has been done within this framework. The translation from standard deviation to the definition that has been used is simply a matter of scale. Regardless of distribution used, Monte Carlo simulation programs provide the standard deviation and the worst-case statistics. It is straightforward to count the number of standard deviations between the average and the worst case. The mechanics of portfolio optimization are scalable as to risk. You can scale after the analysis has been done with one standard deviation, when initially setting up the matrices, as in Table 10.1.

Return is defined as expected return, or the average of distribution of returns as they are calculated in Chapters 4 and 7. Block C combines the risk data with the correlation data, substituting the risk percentages from block A for the lease types in block B. The inner cells of block D show the results of the calculations performed by the elements in block C. To find how the risk of lease A moves with the risk of lease B, multiply the risk of lease A times the correlation coefficient times the risk of lease B. For example: 3% × 0.4 × 5% = 0.0006. On the outer rim of block D are the weights the leases have in the portfolio. In block E the inner cells are calculated by multiplying the proportion of lease A by the covariances between leases A and B, then by the proportion of lease B. For example: 20% × 0.0009 × 38% = 0.0005. With the proportions of each lease and their covariance you can calculate the risk of the portfolio. Risk (standard deviation) is the square root of the sum of the covariances.

Return is calculated by multiplying the weights of each lease in the portfolio by their return. For the proportions shown here, the return is 14.56 percent.

TABLE 10.1   Portfolio Return and Risk

A	Return and Risk Data		
	Lease A	Lease B	Lease C
Return	8%	12%	20%
Risk	3%	5%	10%

B	Correlation Information		
	Lease A	Lease B	Lease C
Lease A	1	0.4	0.5
Lease B	0.4	1	0.2
Lease C	0.5	0.2	1

C	Risk and Correlation Matrix		
	3%	5%	10%
3%	1	0.4	0.5
5%	0.4	1	0.2
10%	0.5	0.2	1

D	Lease Proportions and Covariance Matrix			
		20%	38%	42%
Lease A	20%	0.0009	0.0006	0.0015
Lease B	38%	0.0006	0.0025	0.0010
Lease C	42%	0.0015	0.0010	0.0100

E	Covariance and Risk Calculation			
	Lease A		0.00004	0.00005	0.00010
	Lease B		0.00005	0.00036	0.00016
	Lease C		0.00010	0.00016	0.00176
			0.00020	0.00057	0.00202
	Covariance		0.00279		
	Risk		0.05282		

You want to allocate your portfolio dollars so that the lease combinations produce the best returns for the amount of risk taken. This is done by looking at as many combinations as possible, calculating portfolio risk and return. One approach to finding this frontier is a Monte Carlo simulation that looks at thousands of combinations of leases A, B, and C, then ranks them. The outer border of all of these combinations is called the efficient frontier. Figure 10.1 is an example of 1,000 different combinations. The efficient frontier is the northwestern border of the cluster.

This description has been couched in terms of deciding the proportions of each lease you want to invest in a portfolio. But you can look at this analysis from the perspective of your existing portfolio. The analysis enables you to rank your current portfolio with respect to the efficient frontier. Calculate lease returns, risks, and correlation coefficients with the proportions of your portfolio as in Table 10.1 to find your current risk-return ratio. Then specify risks, returns, and correlation coefficients and allow the lease proportions to vary. This will give you the efficient frontier for the types of leases you have. The calculations are then made on a segment basis. If you

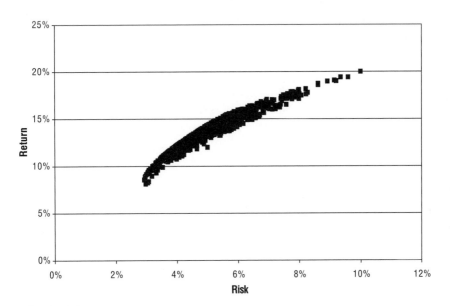

FIGURE 10.1 Efficient Frontier

TABLE 10.2   Portfolio Return and Risk—High Correlation

A	Return and Risk Data		
	Lease A	Lease B	Lease C
Return	8%	12%	20%
Risk	3%	5%	10%

B	Correlation Information		
	Lease A	Lease B	Lease C
Lease A	1	0.8	0.7
Lease B	0.8	1	0.5
Lease C	0.7	0.5	1

are below the frontier, it tells you what you need to do to be at the frontier. That in turn drives your origination and sales strategies.

In Chapter 8 the variability of correlation coefficients was discussed. To show how different correlations can affect portfolio decisions, Table 10.2 reproduces blocks A and B with new and higher correlation coefficients. Any decision about what point on the frontier to choose needs to take account of a possible shift in the correlations.

Figure 10.2 shows that if the leases in the portfolio are more closely correlated, the amount of risk for each unit of return is higher. At a return of 15 percent, the low correlation regime (gray) has risk of 5.4 percent, the high correlation regime (black) has risk of 6.1 percent.

HOW MUCH RISK

The next issue is the criteria for deciding how much risk you want to take. One way to choose the level of risk is to think about the costs and returns. Say your cost of funds is 5 percent. You can choose how much money to invest in leases. In Figure 10.3 a line is drawn from the 5 percent point where you are investing no money in leases to a point, E, where it is tangent with the efficient frontier,

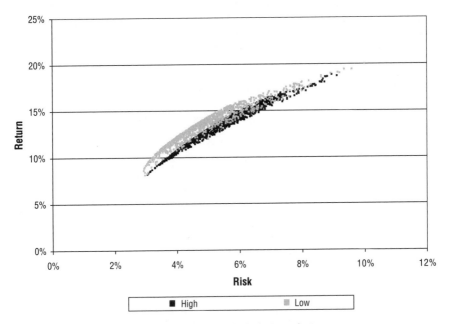

FIGURE 10.2   Efficient Frontiers—Low and High Correlation

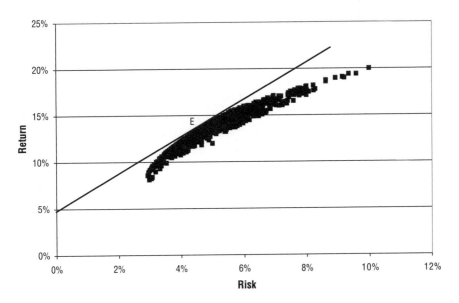

FIGURE 10.3   Choosing a Level of Risk in a Portfolio

at 14 percent. At that point you are fully invested in leases. The lease type combination at that point is A, 21 percent; B, 41 percent, and C, 38 percent. The slope of the line from the 5 percent point to point E is a modified Sharpe ratio. The modification is to substitute a cost of funds rate for a risk-free rate or benchmark rate; the analysis then proceeds along the same path.[3] The ratio is 1.8. You are picking up 1.8 units of return for each unit of risk you take on. The calculation is 14 percent return, less cost of funds rate of 5 percent, divided by the amount of risk, 5 percent. The equation is

$$\text{MSR} = \frac{R - C}{\sigma_P} \tag{10.1}$$

where $\text{MSR} =$ modified Sharpe ratio
$R =$ return
$C =$ cost of funds
$\sigma_P =$ standard deviation of the portfolio

If you move further to the right along the efficient frontier, you pick up more return but more units of risk per unit of return; the slope of the line tangent to the efficient frontier decreases. In the high correlation scenario you only pick up 1.6 units of return for each unit of risk you take on.

Based on an average return of 14 percent, point E, and standard deviation of 5 percent if you invest all of your funds in leases, about 4 percent of the time you will lose money. If the same calculation is applied to these leases in the high correlation regime, you lose money 5 percent of the time.[4] The same calculation can be made for any point on the line. This kind of metric enables you to decide how much risk to accept.

Another approach is to start with your objectives as a business. How much risk do you need to achieve your strategic objectives? For example, your objective might be:

■ Income growth of 15 percent a year.
■ Growth variance of not more than 4 percent in any year.
■ Tax shelter of $400 million a year.

With these objectives, look at the returns and risks of various types of leases and their correlation. The portfolio model approach will tell you the combinations that achieve your objectives at minimum risk.

CONTRIBUTION OF THE NEW LEASE

In Chapter 4 a tool is developed to calculate the risk price of a lease on a stand-alone basis. On its own, a lease may be good, but is it a good lease for your portfolio? That depends on what is in the portfolio. Here are two ways of getting an answer. The first is termed *discrete*; the second, *continuous*.[5] The discrete method is used when there is a large change to the portfolio, a new type of lease, a sizeable increase in an existing portfolio segment, or the acquisition of a new portfolio. The process is to estimate the portfolio with the new contribution, estimate the portfolio without it, then take the difference between the two.

The continuous method is used when there is an incremental change in the position of the portfolio; for example, you add another $5 million to the lease type C segment of the portfolio. It can be readily calculated with the information you have in hand. The risk contribution of the new lease is the sum of the rows of the covariance matrix (block E of Table 10.1) divided by the risk of the portfolio. The equation is:

$$C_C = \frac{(\sigma_C \times \sigma_B \times \rho_{CB} + \sigma_A \times \sigma_C \times \rho_{AC} + \sigma_C \times \sigma_C \times \rho_{CC})}{\sigma_P} \quad (10.2)$$

where C_C = marginal contribution of lease type C to the
portfolio
σ_A = risk of lease A
σ_B = risk of lease B
σ_C = risk of lease C
ρ_{CB} = correlation between leases C and B, and likewise
for pairs AC and CC
σ_P = risk of the portfolio

The contribution of an additional lease C to the risk of the portfolio is 3.86 percent, at the current portfolio weightings, even though lease C's risk on a stand-alone basis is 10 percent. It is worth considering because C's return is 20 percent. The example points out the need to look at risk on both an individual and a portfolio basis prior to making a decision on whether to book a lease.

Figure 10.4 is a representation of the changing contributions to risk of the different leases, going from low to high risk, left to right. At the low-risk end, the low risk lease A is contributing most of the risk to the portfolio. Moving to the right, as the risk and return of the portfolio increase, lease types B and C are added to the portfolio. At the far right, the largest risk, the sole contribution is from lease C. The calculation of risk contribution and how it may change over time reinforces the need to check a new lease against the portfolio. When portfolio risk is in the 5 percent range, lease type C is contributing only 3.86 percent, but as the risk of the portfolio grows, so does its contribution to risk.[6]

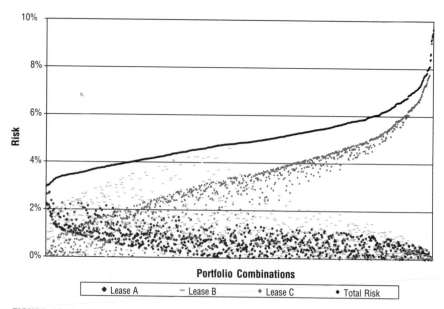

FIGURE 10.4   Contributions to Portfolio Risk

EFFECT OF LUMPINESS

In the previous section, the contribution of a significant addition to your portfolio is handled differently than a small lease. It is worthwhile looking at how a single large risk (one large lease or many small ones with the same characteristics) can affect the outcome of a portfolio.[7] Let's assume that there are two lease portfolios with the same characteristics:

- $1,000,000,000
- 1,000 lessees
- Probability of default 1 percent
- Loss-given-default 30 percent

But there is one significant difference between the two portfolios:

- Lease portfolio A has 1,000 lessees, each with $1,000,000 outstanding.
- Lease portfolio B has 999 lessees, each with $750,000 outstanding, and 1 lessee with $250,750,000 outstanding.

The expected losses in the two portfolios are very different. Using equation (10.3)

$$\text{Expected Loss} = \text{Default Percent} \times \text{Number of Lessees} \times \text{Amount for each Lessee} \times \text{Loss-given-default}$$

for portfolio A:

$$\text{Expected Loss} = \$3,000,000 = 1\% \times 1,000 \times 1,000,000 \times 30\%$$

and for Portfolio B:

$$\text{Expected Loss} = \$3,749,250 = (1\% \times 999 \times 750,000 + 1\% \times 1 \times 250,750,000) \times 30\%$$

Portfolio lumpiness increases expected losses, in this case by 25 percent, and the need for capital in lease portfolios. Large transactions need to be modeled separately and not aggregated.

AN EFFICIENT PORTFOLIO TODAY AND TOMORROW

Leases are long-lived assets. The leases booked today will be around for a number of years, and the secondary market for leases has much less liquidity than the stock or bond market. As a result it is not possible to rebalance your portfolio frequently. A good portfolio model needs to result in an efficient portfolio this year, next year, and into the future. This is the reason that the measurement of the individual risks and the risk pricing tool consider lease cash flows from the beginning to the end of the lease. And you need to have some idea of how to build a portfolio today that will be efficient in the future.

In our example from Table 10.1, you have three types of leases you can put into your portfolio in any proportion. You want to select a program today that will hold for four years and generate a return of at least 15 percent a year, while minimizing the risk in each year. Let's assume each lease type has the same return for the four years: lease A, 8 percent; lease B, 12 percent; lease C, 20 percent. The risks are scheduled to change from year to year because the risks within each lease are changing in importance. And because the risks within the leases are changing, the correlation coefficients between the three types of lease are changing. Table 10.3 has the details.

Because the risks and the correlations are changing, the efficient frontiers in each year will look very different as the relative risks and hence correlation coefficients change. Figure 10.5, on page 162, shows the frontiers for each year. Using a modified Sharpe ratio as the decision tool for each year leaves you with different investment patterns in each year, but not with a solution.

The solution to the multiyear problem is an extension of the way a single year was treated. Set up the matrices as in Table 10.1, one for each year, each year containing its individual risk percentages and correlation coefficients. The extension is to link the investment

TABLE 10.3   Three Leases, Their Risks and Correlations for Four Years

		Year 1					Year 2		
		Risk and Correlation Matrix					Risk and Correlation Matrix		
		Lease A	Lease B	Lease C			Lease A	Lease B	Lease C
		3%	5%	10%			4%	6%	9%
Lease A	3%	1	0.4	0.5	Lease A	4%	1	0.4	0.6
Lease B	5%	0.4	1	0.2	Lease B	6%	0.4	1	0.1
Lease C	10%	0.5	0.2	1	Lease C	9%	0.6	0.1	1
		Year 3					Year 4		
		Risk and Correlation Matrix					Risk and Correlation Matrix		
		Lease A	Lease B	Lease C			Lease A	Lease B	Lease C
		6%	8%	7%			1%	5%	13%
Lease A	6%	1	0.6	0.7	Lease A	1%	1	0.5	0.9
Lease B	8%	0.6	1	−0.2	Lease B	5%	0.5	1	−0.4
Lease C	7%	0.7	−0.2	1	Lease C	13%	0.9	−0.4	1

percentages in each year together. Run the Monte Carlo simulation with each year's risk, return, and investment percentages, view the simulation trials, and select a desired return. You then find the associated risk and investment percentages. Table 10.4 is an example of what the output looks like. A program of investing 7 percent of your funds in lease type A, 52 percent in type B, and 41 percent in type C will generate a 15 percent return each year, with average risk of 5.2 percent.

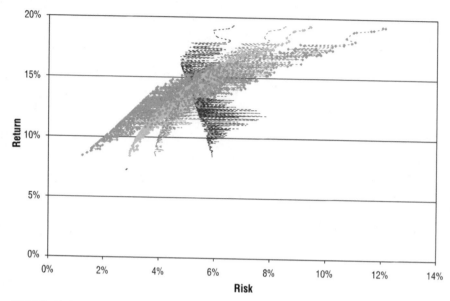

FIGURE 10.5   Efficient Frontiers for Four Years

TABLE 10.4 Sample Output from Monte Carlo Simulation

Year 1		Year 2		Year 3		Year 4		Investment		
Risk	Return	Risk	Return	Risk	Return	Risk	Return	Lease A	Lease B	Lease C
5.41%	15.00%	5.26%	15.00%	4.97%	15.00%	5.01%	15.00%	7%	52%	41%
5.47	15.00	5.29	15.00	4.93	15.00	5.27	15.00	11	46	43
5.61	15.00	5.39	15.00	4.96	15.00	5.74	15.00	17	36	46
5.60	15.01	5.38	15.01	4.95	15.01	5.68	15.01	16	38	46
5.90	15.02	5.67	15.02	5.22	15.02	6.51	15.02	26	23	51
5.51	15.03	5.31	15.03	4.92	15.03	5.38	15.03	12	44	44
5.96	15.03	5.73	15.03	5.28	15.03	6.66	15.03	28	21	52
5.79	15.04	5.55	15.04	5.09	15.04	6.22	15.04	23	28	49
5.98	15.04	5.74	15.04	5.29	15.04	6.69	15.04	28	20	52
5.53	15.04	5.33	15.04	4.92	15.04	5.44	15.04	13	43	44
5.77	15.04	5.53	15.04	5.06	15.04	6.16	15.04	22	29	49
6.04	15.05	5.81	15.05	5.35	15.05	6.83	15.05	29	18	53

Hedging a Leasing Portfolio

You have risk priced the leases in your portfolio; you have looked at the relation of your portfolio to the efficient frontier; you have looked at current and potential lease types to move you closer to the frontier; and you have evaluated and decided to sell some leases from the portfolio, but you are still shy of where you want to be. Solutions are available in the derivative, insurance, and corporate finance markets to decrease risk and increase returns. These same solutions work when you have become overconcentrated in a particular type of risk. This chapter looks at different instruments that focus particularly on credit risk and equipment risk.

CREDIT RISK

There are two basic mechanisms for protecting your portfolio against default by one of your lessees—credit default swaps and factor hedges.[1]

Credit Default Swaps

The most popular instrument for protecting against credit risk is the credit default swap. Credit default swaps are the largest part of the $5 trillion credit derivatives market. The mechanics of a swap are fairly straightforward. You buy protection for a specified period of time by paying a periodic premium to the seller of default protection. If your lessee defaults, you receive a payment. For most major companies, protection is readily available out to 10 years, and can be extended in some instances. The size of the premium depends on the creditworthiness of the lessee you are buying protection against; the spread of its bonds against treasuries is often a good indication. Credit protection is best bought in good times, not bad; premiums rise when trouble looms. The seller of default protection is likely to be a major bank; banks are the principal participants in the market. The term *default* is used to indicate credit events such as bankruptcy, failure to pay, repudiation of debt, acceleration of debt, and restructuring.

There are a couple of variations on the credit default swap that tailor it more to leasing. They relate to:

- The event that triggers payment. As mentioned in the chapter on equipment risk, many lessees view their leased equipment as essential to their operation, so unless they are actually intending to cease operations, they will pay the rent. The standard credit events are not always applicable to your lessee. One variation is to set two triggers, The first may be bankruptcy, the second is failure to pay rent when due. This has the effect of reducing the premium you pay for the protection.

- How the amount of payment is determined. Payment in the credit default swap market is generally calculated as the fall in price of a reference obligation (generally a bond), below par at a predesignated time (for example, 90 days) after the credit event. So if the bond is trading for 60 cents on the dollar, your payment is 40 cents times the amount of protection you bought. But the amount needed to compensate you on the lease may be more or less. You can address this issue ahead of time by specifying the amount of the payment you will receive in event of default. You have the tools to estimate loss-given-default for every year of the lease. These are the payment amounts to specify in the credit default swap agreement.

A credit default swap benefits you by:

- Increasing diversification in the portfolio. Financial institutions are generally the party on the other side of the transaction and they have little correlation with the types of companies that lease equipment.

- Allowing you to do more business with the same lessee. It is a good company, it pays on time, it takes care of the leased equipment; however, your policy is that the exposure to a single lessee will not be more than 2 percent of your portfolio. The premium you pay for the credit default swap needs to be taken into account in calculating the return from new leases. However, the financial institution on the other side of the swap will probably be a better credit risk than your lessee, with a lower probability of default. Therefore, the savings in the amount of capital allocated to the transaction may offset the cost of buying protection, wholly or partially.
- Increasing the credit quality of the portfolio. Before you incur a loss, two events have to occur: The lessee stops paying rent *and* the seller of protection doesn't make the payment.
- Allowing you to maintain control of the lease, and relations with the lessee.
- Remaining off balance sheet. Credit default swaps are shown in the footnotes of financial statements and are not name specific.

There are some drawbacks to credit default swaps:

- For longer leases it may not be possible to match the full maturity of the transaction. Rail, utility, and aircraft leases particularly fall into this category.
- For many smaller lessees credit default swaps aren't available.
- You have a new exposure—to the counterpart in the transaction.

Often lessors shy away from credit default swaps because the premiums seem too high. In addition to tailoring the swap more directly to the lease, premiums can be reduced by offering to take the risk of another company you know—for example, a lessor with whom you would like to do more business. Shown in Figure 11.1, on page 168, is an example where you take the credit risk of lessee B, and in turn the counterpart takes the risk of lessee A. If the two lessees rank equally in terms of creditworthiness, premiums need not be exchanged. A payment occurs only if one of the lessees stops paying rent.

Doing the transaction with another lessor is a way to lengthen

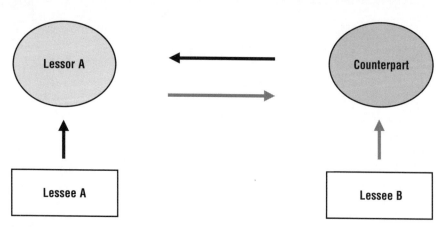

FIGURE 11.1   Credit Default Swap—Trade

the maturity of the swap. It does not depend, as do swaps with the usual bank counterparts, on finding an offset in the bond market. The offset for each party is its own portfolio.

Another alternative to reducing the cost of protection is to buy an option for the right to enter into the credit default swap on a date in the future at a fixed premium on the swap. If the need for protection seems likely, you will have the protection at a premium struck prior to the imminent need. If the need for protection is unlikely, you will have only paid out less money premium than if you had entered into a swap initially. For example, you could enter into a five-year credit default swap today and pay 70 basis points per annum for protection. Or you can pay a fee of 54 basis points for the right to enter into a five-year swap later in which you would pay 80 basis points per annum. The option is a less expensive transaction 95 percent of the time.[2]

Factor Hedges

Rather than buying protection against the default of a lessee, you can buy hedges on the factors that influence or determine whether it will default. The premise for this strategy is that the hedge will increase in value and earn money as the lessee comes close to default.

For airlines the largest expenses are fuel, interest, and labor. Revenues are affected by business conditions, consumer confidence, and competition; for some, foreign exchange rates also have an effect. A number of the factors can be mapped directly to instruments that trade in the market. Jet fuel, interest rates, and foreign exchange rates have active spot, futures, options, and OTC markets. Other factors can be hedged indirectly. Consumer price index futures may be a reasonable proxy for labor costs. The Standard & Poor's (S&P) stock index may be a good proxy for business conditions and consumer confidence. There are stock, futures, and options markets for the S&P index.

The next step is to establish the correlations between the factors and the market instruments. The amount of the hedge of a given factor depends on two things:

1. The impact of the factor on net income. This is determined from the income statements of the lessee over a number of years.
2. The effect of a change in net income on the probability of default. The Moody's KMV Credit Monitor[3] model allows you to simulate changes in income on default probability.

The principal shortfalls of this approach are (1) the fact that most of the market prices are not available for long tenors, and (2) the need to establish the statistical relationships between the prices and the probability of default. The benefit is that it can be used for segments of the portfolio where credit swaps are not available.

EQUIPMENT RISK

The means and markets to hedge equipment risk are much less developed than those for credit. The alternatives that are used include sale of the equipment for future delivery, selling the right for someone else to buy the equipment, entering into remarketing agreements, and buying residual value insurance on the equipment.

Selling the Equipment for Future Delivery

The coal-fired electricity plant in your portfolio does not come off lease until 2025. When the lease was booked in 1995 you were fairly sanguine about the prospects for coal-fired plants; however, the way coal prices have recently tracked natural gas and oil prices has changed your mind. You can arrange to sell the plant to a third party today and receive the proceeds either in 2025 or today. In the first case you have substituted the credit risk of the purchaser for the risk of the value of the plant. And in both cases, you may have to pay taxes today on the proceeds. But calculating the advantages of selling versus holding the equipment to lease end is straightforward.

Selling the Right to Buy the Equipment

You can also sell an option to a third party that specifies that at the end of the lease they receive the proceeds from the sale of the asset above the booked residual, or any other level you may wish to set. Or the transaction may specify levels of participation in the sale proceeds. Above $25 million the lessor receives 70 percent of the next $5 million, 60 percent of the following $5 million, and so on. This transaction gives you income today that effectively reduces your risk in the volatility of the future price of coal-fired electricity plants. The proceeds from the option premium are deducted from the booked value of the equipment in both economic and accounting contexts.

Remarketing Agreements

A variation on this theme is the sale of a remarketing agreement to another lessor.[4] The agreements are structured with a sharing threshold that may be either below, at, or above the level of your booked residual value. The sharing arrangements can be the same as the options. The fee is calculated as the present value of the difference between the threshold and the expected residual value. The calculations are the same as in Chapter 6.

The option and remarketing agreement reduce your risk on the value of the coal-fired plant many years from now; they also allow you to capitalize on today's market expectations of the future value of the plant, which you may not share, and convert the expectations to cash. The treatments of the option premium and remarketing agreement premium for accounting purposes are evolving, so your accountant needs to be consulted.

Buying Residual Value Insurance

Residual value insurance is a popular means of ensuring that the value of the equipment at the end of the lease does not fall below its historical values. This insurance is written below the value cycle of the equipment. Figure 11.2 shows an example of the value cycle of heavy-duty trucks and where the insurance layer is.

Residual value coverage is written with the expectation that if a claim is made and paid, the recoveries from the sale of the trucks will leave the insurer without a loss. Assets that are easily insured have five characteristics:

1. A design and style in common with other equipment of the same type.
2. The latest technology.

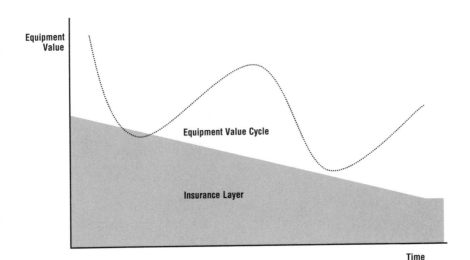

FIGURE 11.2   Basis for Residual Value Insurance on Heavy-Duty Trucks
Source: Thomas A. Orofino, "Structured Indemnities and Asset Based Insurance Enhancements" (presentation, New York, April 1999).

3. Industry standards.
4. Identifiable, liquid secondary markets.
5. Useful lives beyond the end of the lease.[5]

You can readily calculate what you should pay for residual value insurance by using the decay curve and volatility valuation model discussed in Chapter 2. In Chapter 6 you were in the position of selling options to your lessee to buy equipment. Now you are buying an option to sell the equipment to the insurer at a fixed price at the end of the lease. The actual mechanics are different—the equipment is appraised, and you receive a payment for the difference between the insured value and appraised value—but the effect is the same. The calculation of the premium you should pay is

$$RVP = PV \{\max[(IV - E), 0]\} \qquad (11.1)$$

where   RVP = residual value insurance premium
           PV = present value, used because the comparison
                between insured value and actual value is in the
                future, but the insurance premium is paid today
       max = maximum function, which says that if the insured
                value is greater than the equipment value, the
                insurance is valuable to you. If the expression
                $(IV - E)$ is negative, meaning the insured value is
                less than the equipment value, the insurance has
                no value to you.
         IV = insured value
           E = equipment value at lease end

The fleet of trucks has an average estimated value of nearly $300,000. You want to estimate the cost of buying insurance if their value fell below $250,000. Figure 11.3 shows the distribution of the values of the equipment and the insurance premium. The average is the dashed line. The insurance has value only 20 percent of the time since the estimated value of the trucks is below $250,000 only 20 percent of the time. In the area where the insurance is valuable, the premium averages $32,000.

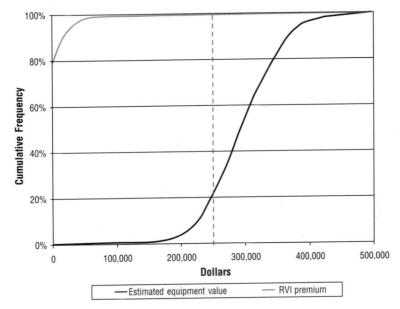

FIGURE 11.3 Equipment Value and Insurance Value

CHAPTER **12**

Portfolio Management in a Leasing Company

A portfolio management group brings the returns and risks of leases together in one place on a common measurement basis. As a result, a lessor is able to determine the lease structures, the types of equipment, the industry sectors, and the lessees that contribute most to its bottom line and to take account of the risk they bring with them.

BUSINESS MODEL

There are a number of business models for portfolio management. Starting with the activities assigned to portfolio management, the models spell out the responsibilities of the group, as shown in Table 12.1, on page 176.[1]

The business model favored here is model 3. The reason for not moving entirely to model 4, where portfolio management has sole responsibility for the bottom line, is that it is desirable to have the people that source transactions continue to have an interest in the outcome of the transactions they initiate.

In keeping with this model for portfolio management, it is useful to think of your portfolio as an investor who seeks to maximize return on the risk you take. The portfolio is guided by the return/risk maxim, "Get paid for the risk you take." The portfolio follows the maxim regardless of your other activities as the lessor—originating new business, serving the customer base, or maintaining specific credit levels. The role of portfolio management is to maximize risk-

TABLE 12.1 Business Models for Portfolio Management

	Model 1	Model 2	Model 3	Model 4
Portfolio Management Activities	Monitor and report	Monitor and report *plus* hedge and sell existing exposure to reduce risk or increase diversification	Monitor and report *plus* hedge, sell, and *buy* exposure. Actively manage the portfolio within parameters	Monitor and report *plus* hedge, sell, and *buy* exposure. Actively manage the portfolio *to maximize income.*
Owner of the Portfolio	Origination	Origination	Portfolio management	Portfolio management
Owner of the Profit & Loss Statement	Origination	Origination, with shadow P&L for portfolio management	Origination and portfolio management	Portfolio management

Origination is the group that brings in new lease transactions and structures with a view of the customer's objectives and the objectives of the leasing company. Origination may also include the underwriting group that analyzes credit and equipment and assigns a rating to the risk of the transaction.

Source: Alexandre Santos, "Overcoming Challenges to Implementing Active Portfolio Management Activities" (presentation, Global Association of Risk Professionals, New York, May 2003).

adjusted return and communicate with and direct other groups in the leasing company in fulfilling its objective.

KEY CONCEPTS

All investors have basic principles that they follow. These basic principles are adapted for lessors.

- The keys to long-term profitability and viability are economic return, risk, and their relationship.
- The risks of a lease transaction over its life should be understood and quantified. The result will be a lease that is better priced and structured, and it will be more profitable.
- The risks and returns in the portfolio should be understood and quantified. The result is that you as a portfolio manager will know what kinds of leases you want more of, what to keep, and what to sell.
- Each lease that is originated should be able to be sold to one of two markets—into the lessor's own portfolio or to the larger world of investors (other lessors, banks, mutual funds).
- The execution of portfolio strategies developed by the portfolio management group depends on a team. Portfolio management depends on originators, underwriters, equipment specialists, and specialists in buying and selling leases. There are a number of strategies for changing the return/risk mix of your portfolio, but as mentioned in Chapter 11, very few can be executed by picking up the phone and making a call.

FUNCTIONS

The portfolio management group achieves its objectives by:

- Telling the people in origination the criteria for leases that will be accepted into the portfolio and those that will not be. The syndications group tells the people in origination the criteria for leases that can be sold to other investors and those that cannot be.

- Knowing and tracking the effect of changing economic, financial, and political conditions on the portfolio.
- Knowing and tracking the effect of changing prices on the financial health of lessees.
- Obtaining information from the equipment group to understand how much the equipment is worth if the lessee defaults on its rent payments.
- Actively monitoring lessees, identifying problems, and intervening early.
- Communicating with the people in the syndications group about the leases that portfolio management wants to sell in the secondary market, receiving feedback from syndications on the price these leases can be sold at, and deciding to accept the price or continue to hold the lease in portfolio.
- Executing derivative transactions to mitigate credit, equipment, and tax risk.
- Buying secondary market leases or other financial instruments to improve the risk-adjusted return profile of the portfolio.

The rest of this chapter expands on these objectives and functions.

RISK-ADJUSTED RETURNS

One of the shortcomings of lessors, as well as of banks and funds management firms, is that they traditionally divide risk and return into two separate processes. One group looks only at returns, the other focuses only on risk. There are problems with this approach. The problem with a return focus is that a lot of risk can get added for a small amount of return. Also, a return focus ignores techniques such as adding returns by originating leases that are not highly correlated with other risks in the portfolio. The problem with a risk focus is that most of the attention is on minimizing it, to the detriment of return. Getting paid for risk won't be part of the consideration if return is not part of the equation. The problem with long-lived leases is that the risks and returns are changing over their lives. The portfolio manager needs to know whether the return covers the risk.

ORGANIZATION

The suggested organizational structure of a leasing company that highlights portfolio management is shown in Table 12.2. This structure follows from model 3 recommended earlier in the chapter and from key investment concepts and functions of the portfolio management group.

The *portfolio management committee* centralizes decision making and responsibility for achieving portfolio goals and objectives within the broader view of serving lessees and meeting the lessor's current financial objectives. The committee sets company-wide policies and provides guidance to line units.

Origination meets with customers, brings in new lease transactions, and structures them with a view of the customers' objectives and the objectives of the lessor they work for.

The *underwriting credit* section examines the financials of a potential lessee in the context of relevant economic, regulatory, and political factors, and decides how a potential lessee should be rated (its probability of default).

The *underwriting equipment* section considers what the lessee will do with the equipment, the conditions in the lease agreement, and what the current and future markets for the equipment are like. It sets a residual value for the equipment. Ongoing, the equipment function keeps tabs on equipment markets, compares the equipment

TABLE 12.2 Organization of the Lessor Company

			Portfolio Management Committee ↑
Origination	Underwriting	Markets	Portfolio Management
Sales	Credit	Leases	Analysis
Structuring	Equipment	Derivatives	Monitor
			Pricing

in the portfolio to the market, and keeps portfolio management abreast of changes in equipment values.

Markets works outside of the leasing company to do what cannot be done inside of it. It is the tool of the origination and portfolio management sectors. Markets' role is to sell or hedge risk that you do not want. Markets also buys new and seasoned leases and executes derivative transactions that improve the return\risk profile of the portfolio. The people involved in lease markets sell leases that are initiated by the origination sector, but which do not fit, in whole or in part, in the lessor's portfolio. They also sell seasoned leases that portfolio management wishes to dispose of. They buy new and seasoned leases from other lessors to add to the portfolio.

Portfolio management communicates with origination, underwriting, and markets on the basis of return and risk. For example, they may state "For a three-year lease to a financial institution on computer equipment, the risk-adjusted return on capital (RAROC) must be at least 17 percent." The return target takes into account the portfolio diversification effects of computer equipment relative to all other equipment in the portfolio, and the correlation between financial institutions and other industries in the portfolio. Clarity about the portfolio's appetites allows people in origination and markets to focus their efforts more tightly, saves time, and allows them to initiate or buy leases that will be booked, not rejected.

Through the markets group, portfolio management sells single leases or bundles of them that have been in the portfolio. The reasons are many—to increase income in the current period, to reduce the risk of a single lessee or a group of them, to reduce concentration in an industry or factor, to reduce risk in a particular equipment type, or to make room for a new, more attractive lease.

ANALYTICAL TOOLS

To execute its responsibilities, portfolio management should have a number of formal analytical tools at its disposal. The value of a formal set of tools is that they

- Create a disciplined approach to problems.
- Allow you to quantify assumptions that can be quantified.

- Communicate with everyone in the leasing company in a standard way.

But the tools are neither a substitute for common sense nor to be used to make the final decision. Think about what you did not or could not include in the numerical analysis. These elements need to be combined with the results of the quantitative analysis to reach a final decision.

The basic tool set includes:

- Risk-based pricing. It estimates the risk-adjusted return of an individual lease (see Chapter 4).
- Lease valuation. It indicates the value of holding versus the value of selling a lease on both economic and accounting bases (see Chapter 7).
- Factor analysis. It provides an early warning signal about lessee and industry financial health (see Chapter 9).
- Portfolio model. This is the basic tool for deciding which leases are desirable and which are not (see Chapter 10).

INTEGRATED PORTFOLIO MANAGEMENT

Though the basic communication from portfolio management to the rest of the leasing company is on the basis of return and risk, that is not sufficient. There are additional practices and philosophies that are the hallmarks of good portfolio management. These practices effectively focus the entire leasing company on portfolio management. A number of them are discussed here.[2]

Lessons Learned

This is a write-up about a lease where the lessor lost money, had serious problems, or there was a near miss (a problem popped up but was successfully resolved). The reason for the write-up is so you will not have to learn the lesson again, and, in the case of near misses, it illustrates how a particular structure protected the lessor. The write-up highlights the reasons for the loss or problems with the transaction and points to issues that might have been identified before the lease was first booked. In addition, it alerts everyone to new issues to be aware of in originating new leases and monitoring the portfolio. It also talks about elements that were in the lease contract, or might have been, to mitigate the loss. The write-up is widely distributed within the leasing company.

Origination and Buying Guidelines

In addition to return and risk guidelines, a lessor should have a clear definition of the industries and equipment markets it wants to be involved in. Even though "Know thy customer" is a familiar maxim, the financial landscape is strewn with lenders who have not heeded it. The same maxim applies to industries and equipment types. No lessors can be knowledgeable about all industries or all equipment types, so it pays to specialize. The guidance applies equally to newly originated leases, new and seasoned leases bought from others, and derivatives.

The caveat is that specialization should not lead to a lack of diversification. Portfolio management has the responsibility of examining the relationships between the factors that drive industries and equipment to ensure that they are not highly correlated, even in periods of economic and financial crisis.

Equipment Guidelines

If the equipment is both essential to the operation and produces revenue for the lessee, the equipment will most likely be maintained, and even when the lessee encounters financial problems it will generally continue to pay rent. The experience of a number of lessors confirms this. The computers that run the reservation system of an airline and the phone systems that link reservation agents are examples of equipment that is essential and revenue producing. Planes might seem to fulfill both requirements; however, a reduction in routes and new competition can create excess capacity; then the plane becomes nonessential.

Early Warning Systems

Early warning systems are essential for portfolio management. They allow management to intervene early in an attempt to exit the lease or shore up its position and minimize its losses. This involves verification that all documentation is in order and that the lessee is complying with *all* the terms and conditions of the lease contract, particularly maintenance provisions. Noncompliance may give the lessor the ability to accelerate payment of rents or return of the equipment. The people in portfolio management responsible for monitoring sets of accounts rely on a number of indicators. Among the tools are:

- *Factor analysis.* This is a tool that uses market prices and indices to forecast changes in the cost and revenue structure of industries and companies. See Chapter 9 for more detail.
- *Industry analysis.* This analysis describes the current state of an industry. It lays out the driving cost and revenue factors in an industry. It explains the critical issues facing the industry, such as increased regulation. The analysis addresses the competitive environment, not only within the industry but from outside as well. It talks of the opportunities for the growth of the industry and forecasts future prospects.
- *Tracking stock prices.* The stock price of a company, when compared to the movement of the overall market, encapsulates the reactions of a large number of people to news about the company. Day-to-day movements are erratic; a trend away from the market, particularly a downward movement, calls for deeper investigation of the lessee.
- *Estimates of default probability.* Moody's KMV Expected Default Frequencies (EDF)[3] are forward-looking default probabilities for public and private companies. Public company EDF credit measures are based on extracting collective, real-time intelligence from global markets. A public company's probability of default is calculated from three drivers—the market value of its assets, its volatility, and its current capital structure. For each company, the EDF credit measure captures the credit insight from the equity market and combines it with a picture of the company's current capital structure. For private companies, fundamental data are lined up with observations of default to capture the predictors and their impact on default.
- *Online news.* Dow Jones News Retrieval[4] transmits more than 3,000 items on busy days. It features corporate developments,

U.S. and Canadian equity market news, U.S. economic news and indicators, and global geopolitical and economic news. Filters can be set up to track specific companies and industries.

- *Dun & Bradstreet Alert Services.*[5] The service is particularly useful for small, privately owned, nonrated lessees. It is a business monitoring service that allows lessors to choose from 13 elements to monitor the lessees they have registered with D&B. The elements include bankruptcy filings, PAYDEX score, public records, and UCC filings. You can select the frequency of notification, from daily to monthly, and the delivery method—on line, e-mail, or fax.

EXAMPLES OF INTEGRATED PORTFOLIO MANAGEMENT

In this section there are three examples of how portfolio management works with the other groups in the leasing company to execute portfolio objectives. In Figure 12.1 action is triggered by portfolio management's early warning systems. Factor analysis identifies that

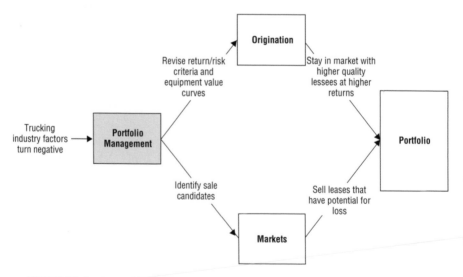

FIGURE 12.1   Factor Analysis Triggers Action
Source: Ronald Chamides and Beverly Davis, "Total Risk Management, Strategic Risk Management at Fleet Capital Leasing" (presentation, Providence, RI, January 1998).

diesel prices and insurance premiums for the trucking industry have been on an upward path for the last six months and there are no apparent reasons the trends will not continue for some time. The diagram traces subsequent responses with the leasing company.

In the second example (Figure 12.2), the equipment group observes that the market for coal cars is strengthening. Both new and used cars are increasing in price. One of the principal car manufacturers has decided to exit the business, and coal is increasingly being substituted for natural gas.

The third example (Figure 12.3, on page 186) shows how portfolio management and the other groups in the leasing company react to a new market opportunity. The first step is to understand the lessee industry or industries and the equipment they will be leasing. Only then does origination proceed.

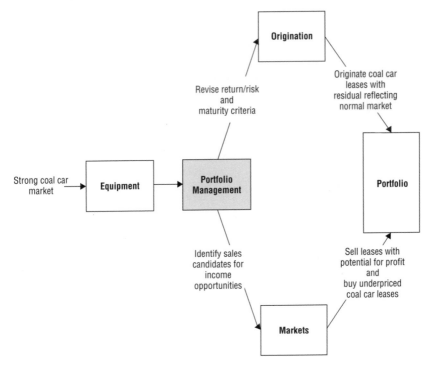

FIGURE 12.2 Movement in Equipment Prices Triggers Action
Source: Ronald Chamides and Beverly Davis, "Total Risk Management, Strategic Risk Management at Fleet Capital Leasing" (presentation, Providence, RI, January 1998).

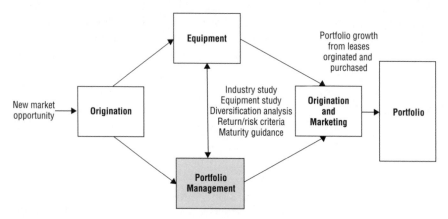

FIGURE 12.3 New Market Opportunity Triggers Action
Source: Ronald Chamides and Beverly Davis, "Total Risk Management, Strategic Risk Management at Fleet Capital Leasing" (presentation, Providence, RI, January 1998).

MEASURING PERFORMANCE

The principal measures of performance follow directly from the responsibilities of portfolio management. The first two measures are the amount of return from the portfolio (modified by the amount and number of new leases origination is able to initiate) and the amount of risk taken to generate the return. In financial statement terms, return is the amount of after-tax income after reserves; risk is the amount of capital.

The performance measures are applied to the portfolio as a whole, for each industry segment, for each factor, and for each lessee. The ratio of income to capital for each segment of the portfolio should be at least equal to, if not greater than, the lessor's overall target. This target can be imposed on each segment of the portfolio because when you calculate the amount of capital, the diversification effects of the portfolio segment are taken into account. Chapter 10 discusses this fully.

The performance measures are applied to the portfolio and the segment in a normal operating environment and also in a stressed environment. The stressed environments are the scenarios in the tails of the distributions characterized by regime change. Recall the discussion in Chapter 3. The reason for measuring the segments in a stressed environment is to determine whether one single segment can materially harm the portfolio. The segment can just as easily be a single lessee as an entire industry segment.

The third measure for portfolio management is the degree of diversification in the portfolio. The degree of diversification is readily assessed by looking at the difference between the amount of capital that would be required if all risks were perfectly correlated and the amount in your diversified portfolio. As before, diversification should be measured in both normal and stressed environments.

The fourth measure for portfolio management is the percentage of losses and classified assets in the portfolio. Even if the income to capital ratio is high, a high loss or classified percentage has traditionally forecast trouble ahead. Those circumstances suggest that the algorithms measuring risk and the numbers being put into them may need to be modified.

Notes

CHAPTER 1   What a Lease Looks Like

1. Global Insight Advisory Services Group, *The Benefits of Leasing—Value and Market Perceptions*, cited in *ELT*, June/July 2004, 34.
2. For this table on lease cash flows and others in the book, the Warren & Selbert ABC pricing system is used.
3. A disclaimer: The companies that are mentioned may or may not lease this or any other type of equipment. The equipment types and companies are used for illustration only. The credit ratings are public information provided by Standard & Poor's.

CHAPTER 2   Equipment Risk

1. The road and highway construction index is from the U.S. Census Bureau, sourced at www.economagic.com. The producer price indices are sourced from the U.S. Department of Labor, Bureau of Labor Statistics, available at www.bls.gov/ppi/home.htm. All the time series are monthly; year-to-year changes are calculated by comparing the same month in subsequent years.
2. The Myerson distribution was developed by Roger B. Myerson. A description is found in Roger B. Myerson, *Probability Models for Economic Decisions* (Chicago: Thomson Books/Cole, 2005), pages 122–124. Myerson formulates a family of generalized-lognormal distributions with three parameters of the form $c \times X + d$, where X is a normal or lognormal random variable and c and d are nonrandom constants. This form of distribution is particularly applicable for estimating equipment prices since there is no need to make an *a priori* judgment about how the data are distributed.
3. The simulations used in the book are performed with a Monte Carlo simulation program called XLSim.xla from AnalyCorp Inc. The program is easy to use, intuitive, and quick for these kinds of calculations. Information is available at www.analycorpinc.com.

4. Sam Savage, "The Flaw of Averages," *The San Jose Mercury News*, October 8, 2000. Available on the Web at http://www.stanford.edu/~savage/flaw/Article.htm.

5. The Myerson distribution formula is one of the distribution alternatives in XLSim.xla. The logic behind this model is incorporated in the Equipment Valuation Model developed by APERIMUS. A description can be found on the Web at www.aperimus.com.

6. Producer price indices are available on the Web at www.bls.gov/ppi/home.htm.

7. The combine data is provided with permission by F.A.C.T.'s Report. It compiles auction price data on farm and construction equipment sold throughout North America. Available on the Web at www.machinerypete.com.

8. David C. Rode, P.C. Dunway, P.S Fishbeck, and S.R. Dean, "Inferring Individual Asset Values from Aggregate Transaction Data," *The Appraisal Journal*, October 2002, 417–425. The article contains a detailed description on ways to adjust data series. The referenced equipment is power plants.

9. Some of the ideas for this model came from working with Bob Mercogliano, Siemens Financial Services, and Bengt Hagstrom, General Electric Capital Corporation.

10. A sophisticated analytical software package with a complete set of statistics is SPSS 11.5 for Windows.

11. Bradley Efron and Robert J. Tibshirani, *An Introduction to the Bootstrap* (New York: Chapman & Hall, 1993).

12. The bootstrap function contained in Crystal Ball, a Monte Carlo simulation software package developed by Decisioneering, Inc., works well.

CHAPTER 3 Credit Risk

1. Moody's Investors Service, *Default & Recovery Rates of Corporate Bond Issuers* (New York: Moody's Investors Service, annual); Standard & Poor's, *Annual Global Corporate Default Study: Corporate Defaults Poised to Rise in 2005* (New York: Standard & Poor's, 2005).

2. David T. Hamilton, *Default & Recovery Rates of Corporate Bond Issuers* (New York: Moody's Investors Service, 2005), 16.

3. Ibid., 22–32.

4. Credit Monitor was developed by KMV; CreditMetrics, by JP Morgan; CreditRisk+, by Credit Suisse First Boston; and Risk Manager, by Kamakura.

5. A more complete description of Credit Monitor can be found in Peter J. Crosbie and Jeffrey R. Bohn, *Modeling Default Risk* (San Francisco: KMV, 2002).

6. Adapted from Crosbie and Bohn, 11.

7. A more complete description of CreditMetrics can be found in Greg M. Gupton et al., *CreditMetrics—Technical Document* (New York: JP Morgan & Company, 1997, 5–33. The book is available on the Web at www.riskmetrics.com.

8. A more complete description of CreditRisk+ can be found in Credit Suisse First Boston, *CreditRisk+, A Credit Risk Management Framework* (London: Credit Suisse First Boston International, 1997, 3–22. Available on the Web at www.csfb.com/institutional/research/assets/creditrisk.pdf.

9. A more complete description of the Kamakura models can be found in Kamakura Corporation, KRIS™ Kamakura Risk Information Services, *Kamakura Public Firm Models*, Version 3.0 (2004). Available on the Web at www.kamakuraco.com/DOCS/KRIS-PublicFirm-DPM-usA2.pdf. The equations and their explanations are from Donald R. van Deventer, Kenji Imai, and Mark Mesler, *Advanced Financial Risk Management: Tools and Techniques for Integrated Credit Risk and Interest Rate Risk Management* (unpublished: January 2004), 5–6.

10. This section is paraphrased from Philip Lowe, "Credit Risk Measurement and Procyclicality," *BIS Working Papers*, 116 (2002), 2–3.

11. Hamilton, *Default and Recovery Rates*, 36.

12. Reported by Roberto Violi, "Credit Ratings Transition in Structured Finance," *CGFS Working Group on Ratings in Structured Finance*, December 2004, 8–9.

13. Gupton et al., *CreditMetrics*, 65–76.

14. Lowe, "Credit Risk Management and Procyclicality," 6 and Darrell Duffie and Kenneth J. Singleton, *Credit Risk* (Princeton: Princeton University Press, 2003), 95–99.

15. This formulation for momentum is suggested by the work of Caginalp and Constantine on the stock market. Gunduz Caginalp and George Constantine, "Statistical Inference and Modeling of Momentum in Stock Prices," *Applied Mathematical Finance 2* (1995), 225–242.

16. For more on regime change and a complete mathematical description see Kent Osband, *Iceberg Risk* (New York: Texere, 2002) 45–87 and 148–163. Also see Mary Hardy, "A Different Kind of Regime Switching," *Financial Engineering News*, (January/February 2005), 15–18.

17. Roger J. Bos, Kevin Kelhoffer, and David Keisman, *Ultimate Recovery in an Era of Record Defaults* (New York: Standard & Poor's, July 2002), 2–6.

18. Hamilton, *Default and Recovery Rates*, 6.

19. These formulations and scenarios are an expression of the U.S. bankruptcy code and provisions commonly found in lease contracts. Some of the formulations were developed by the author and others at Bank of America and Montrose & Company. They are used with permission of Bank of America and Montrose. See also William B. Piels, "Lessor Damages and Mitigation" (presentation to Equipment Leasing Association Large Ticket Conference, April 2003).

CHAPTER 4   A Tool for Risk Pricing Leases

1. The development of this risk pricing tool has benefited significantly from discussions in recent years with Julie Fellows-Mason, Ron Ginochio, Bob Purcell, and Chuck Sellman.

CHAPTER 5   Tax Risk

1. Internal Revenue Service, *Corporation Income TaxBrackets & Rates, 1909–2002*, 1993, 284–290. Available on the Web at www.irs.org.
2. This trinomial model is a generalization of one developed by Jenny Malitsky for tax risk at Bank of America in 1997.

CHAPTER 6   Options in a Lease

1. The discussion on the valuation of an early buyout option has benefited from a number of discussions with Ron Ginochio in recent years.
2. This model generally follows the Cox-Ingersoll-Ross model for interest rates. J. C. Cox, J. E. Ingersoll, and S. A. Ross, "A Theory of Term Structure of Interest Rates," *Econometrica 53* (1985), 385–407.

CHAPTER 7   Lease Returns

1. This material in this section is largely based on a seminar conducted by the author at The Leasing Exchange Portfolio Management Conference, Phoenix, October 1998.

CHAPTER 8   Diversification

1. Sections of this chapter are adapted from an article by the author, "Risks and Returns in a Portfolio of Leases," *Journal of Equipment Lease Finance* (2001), and from a presentation by the author titled

"The Value of Diversification" (presentation to The Leasing Exchange Forum, Salt Lake City, February 1999).

2. John Zerolis, "Keys to Visualizing Correlation and Volatility" (presentation to Portfolio Analytics Conference, New York, December 1996).

3. Chapter 9 contains a fuller discussion of the uses of factor analysis.

4. Gupton et al., *CreditMetrics*, 90–94 (see chap. 3 n. 7).

5. Ibid., 98–101.

6. The CreditMetrics program for generating asset correlations is easy to use. The underlying data is updated weekly. See www.riskmetrics.com for further information.

7. Some of the better known data suppliers are:

   Aircraft: Avitas at www.avitas.com and Air Claims at www.airclaimsv1.com.

   Rail: Rail Solutions at www.railsolutionsinc.com.

   Equipment and machinery: Heavy Equipment Sales at www.heavy-equipment-sales.com, Iron Solutions at www.ironsolutions.com, and AccuVal at www.accuval.net.

8. Producer price indices are sourced from the U.S. Department of Labor, Bureau of Labor Statistics, available on the Web at www.bls.gov/ppi/home.htm.

9. A good introduction to copulas is Kevin Dowd, "An Informal Introduction to Copulas," *Financial Engineering News*, March/April 2004, 15, 20.

10. Bill Ziemba, "The Stochastic Programming Approach to Managing Hedge and Pension Fund Risk, Disasters, and their Prevention," *Wilmott magazine*, 2004, 8–16.

11. Kenrick R. M. Ramlochan, "Forecasting Correlations Using Implied Volatilities," *Bank of America Foreign Exchange Monograph Series 88* (1997); K. J. Forbes and R. Rigobon, "No Contagion, Only Interdependence: Measuring Stock Market Comovements," *Journal of Finance 57* (October 2002), 2223–2261; Henri J. Bernard and Gabriele E. B. Galati, "The Co-movement of U.S. Stock Markets and the Dollar," *BIS Quarterly Review*, (January 2002) 31–34.

12. This illustration follows that of Sam Savage, *Decision Making with Insight*, (Belmont: Brooks/Cole, 2003), 89.

CHAPTER 9   Factor Analysis

1. *Factor analysis* is also the name of a formal statistical procedure whose objective is to mathematically determine a few factors, out of a large

set, that are important in explaining some phenomena. This chapter is a derivation of the more formal analysis.

2. Allan Malz, "Crises and Volatility," *Risk*, November 2001, 105–108.

3. The U.S. Census Bureau lists all the codes on the Web at http://www .census.gov/epcd/www/naicstab.htm.

4. The Bureau of Economic Analysis web site is www.bea.gov.

CHAPTER 10   Portfolio Risk and Return

1. The basic works on portfolio theory are Harry Markowitz, *Portfolio Selection: Efficient Diversification of Investments* (New York: John Wiley & Sons, Inc.; 1959), and William F. Sharpe, *Portfolio Theory and Capital Markets* (New York: McGraw-Hill, 1970).

2. This example follows Sharpe 43–44.

3. William F. Sharpe, "The Sharpe Ratio," *The Journal of Portfolio Management*, Fall 1994, 49–58.

4. A Monte Carlo simulation of normal distribution with a mean of 14 percent and a standard deviation of 5 percent with 10,000 trials was run. All of the investment was lost 0.33 percent of the time.

5. Ugur Koyluoglu and Jim Stoker, "Honor Your Contribution," *Risk*, April 2002, 90–94.

6. A refinement on the contribution calculation is the identification of which lease is contributing most to risk in the tail of the distribution. The hypothesis is that the contribution to risk is not proportional throughout the risk distribution. An approach to identifying the significant contributors is contained in Jack Praschnik, Gregory Hayt, and Armand Principato, "Calculating the Contribution," *Risk*, October 2001, S25–S27.

7. This section follows a paper by Mike Fadil, "Size Matters: An Illustration on Oversized Positions and Their Impact on Capital" (presentation to FleetBoston Financial, Boston, November 2001).

CHAPTER 11   Hedging a Lease Portfolio

1. Some of the information for the credit risk section is drawn from *The JP Morgan Guide to Credit Derivatives* (London: Risk Publications, 1999); Sue Noack, Chris Woolley, and Don Young, "Hedging Credit Risk" (presentation to The Leasing Exchange Portfolio Management Conference, Phoenix, October 2000); and *The Lehman Brothers Guide to Exotic Credit Derivatives* (London: RiskWaters Group, 2003).

2. Indicative prices are based on market quotes and estimates of option prices contained in John Hull and Alan White, "The Valuation of

Credit Default Swap Options" (January 2003). Available on the Web at defaultrisk.com/rs_while_alan.htm.
3. Information on Credit Monitor can be found on the Web at www .moodyskmv.com/product/company_creditmonitor.html. The basics of the model are described in Chapter 3.
4. Based on Andrew Loft, "Generating Income from a Mature Lease Portfolio" (presentation to the Equipment Leasing Association Annual Convention, San Diego, October 2003).
5. Based on Thomas A. Orofino, "Structural Indemnities and Asset Based Insurance Enhancements" (presentation, New York, April 1999).

CHAPTER 12 Portfolio Management in a Leasing Company

1. This table was adapted from Alexandre Santos, "Overcoming Challenges to Implementing Active Portfolio Management Activities" (presentation to Global Association of Risk Professionals (GARP), 2003), 11.
2. These sections borrow extensively from Ronald Chamides and Beverly Davis, "Total Risk Management, Strategic Risk Management at Fleet Capital Leasing" (presentation, Providence, RI, January 1998).
3. Further information on Moody's KMV Expected Default Frequencies is available on the Web at www.moodyskmv.com/product/company _credit monitor.html. The basics of the model are described in Chapter 3. This description is paraphrased from this source.
4. Further information on Dow Jones News Service is available on the Web at www.dowjonesnews.com.
5. Further information on Alert Services from Dun & Bradstreet is available on the Web at http://dnb.com/us/dbproducts/risk_manage_portfolio/ alert_.

Bibliography

Bluhm, Christian, Ledger Overbeck, and Christoph Wagner. *An Introduction to Credit Risk Modeling.* Boca Raton: Chapman & Hall/CRC, 2003.

Gupton, Greg M., Christopher C. Finger, and Mickey Bhatia. *CreditMetrics—Technical Document.* New York: J.P. Morgan & Company, 1997.

Osband, Kent. *Iceberg Risk.* New York: Texere, 2002.

Savage, Sam L. *Decision Making with Insight.* Belmont: Brooks/Cole, 2003.

Sharpe, William F. *Portfolio Theory and Capital Markets.* New York: McGraw-Hill, 1970.

Statsoft. *Electronic Statistics Textbook.* Available on the web at www.statsoft.com/textbook/stfacan.html.

Walker, Townsend. "Risks and Returns in a Portfolio of Leases." *Journal of Equipment Lease Finance* (Fall 2002).

Index